ON MY HONOR
I WILL DO MY BEST

ON MY HONOR I WILL DO MY BEST

A Memoir of Making the Most of What Comes Our Way

BILL DEFFEBACH

Library of Congress Number: 2004095160
ISBN: Hardcover 1-4134-6190-5
Softcover 1-4134-6189-1

This book was printed in the United States of America.

To order additional copies of this book, contact:
Xlibris Corporation
1-888-795-4274
www.Xlibris.com
Orders@Xlibris.com
25868

Contents

APPENDIX

Preface

Life is like a bowl of soup. The aroma and taste of good soup depend not only upon its basic ingredients, but also on how you season and cook it. Life's soup is no different; its result also depends on the basic ingredients (genes and environment) and seasoning (skill, common sense, values and grace) that are in the blend. In addition, the final result of life's soup is also dependent on how it is cooked. In this context, cooking means how you *play the game.*

In life's game, it is extremely important to remember that one does not have the luxury of standing on the sidelines just watching life go by. Nor should one depend on luck. How many people do you know who made a fortune in Las Vegas or by winning a lottery? And of those you read about who did, how many let their *easy money* slip through their hands due to their lack of fundamental skills and values?

Accordingly, everybody needs to take active charge of their life and make the best of the opportunities that come their way. Most successful people I have known did not sit on the sidelines or depend on luck. They *cooked* life the old-fashioned way by working hard, earning their own way, developing acumen by learning *something* from each experience in life, good or bad; and then giving something back to their community, church, charities and those in need. Don't go through life by receiving only; be sure to throw something back since the real measure of success is a person's investment in eternity.

My *soup* has been cooking for seventy-three years, and there has been a lot of seasoning added during that time.

Rather than leave the recipe entirely to the uncertainty of word-of-mouth transmission, I am writing this book. Of course, it's primarily for the benefit of future and mostly unknown generations of my descendants. There may be others who will find it of some interest or practical use, as a number of my associates have been after me for some time to put the highlights of my professional and business experiences in print. These tales may not always be typical of the times in which they take place, and thus they may not be completely representative of the history of the last three quarters of a century. However, they do contain slices of that history that happened on my watch; and I hope that something in the recipe I am leaving will be of value to those who follow me.

My bowl of life's *soup* was greatly influenced by my roots, genes and those inherent values instilled in me by my grandparents and parents. Regardless of one's brand or denomination of religion, it is important to instill in our children fundamental beliefs in God and ethical values. This should be basic training, as they will have choices to make, from time to time, as they encounter *forks in life's roads* they travel, and which require a fundamental knowledge of what is right and wrong in order to make the right decision. A simple illustration that everyone can relate to is to recall the first time a cashier made a mistake and gave you more change back than you had coming. If you were lucky enough to be raised with the values my parents and grandparents instilled in me, the choice to return the overpayment is automatic. Otherwise, I could not have lived with my own *conscience*, and it would have deviled me with many sleepless nights and regrets. Whatever personal beliefs one has or does not have at the time a child is brought into this world, it makes common sense in either case to afford one's offspring an *opportunity to develop a conscience* by exposure to this basic training. What better way can a loving and caring mother and father ensure their children will choose the right road at its *forks in life*?

On the other side of the ledger, no one promised me a

rose garden; and my major disappointment is that I am not universally loved within my own family and I have a thorn or two with which I reluctantly have to live. The good and bad news will be covered in these chapters. I am grateful, however, for the love and affection of my wife, Carolyn, and my other immediate and extended family members who have been there for me over the years. I have also been extremely lucky to have had many close friends, professional and business partners, as well as other associates who contributed to the enjoyment of the full life God has given me. Moreover, many of these partners and associates are in the close-friend category as well.

Although I retired on February 2, 2003 (my seventy-second birthday), it has been easy to remain active because I realize there is still a lot to learn. When I awaken each morning, I give thanks because every day, minute and breath thereafter is a gift from God.

Bill Deffebach
Houston, Texas
July 4, 2004

Chapter I

ROOTS

I think that everyone should have as much information about their ancestry as reasonably possible. For years I did not know much about the family, except we were of German descent on my dad's side and English on my mom's. My grandparents and parents had told me at various times that my dad's family had come from the Black Hills area of South Dakota; and that my great-grandfather had been killed by the Indians. When I was in high school, our family took a vacation trip to that area and visited his grave site in Moriah Cemetery located in Deadwood, South Dakota. Was I ever impressed as it was situated within yards of the grave sites of Wild Bill Hickok and Calamity Jane! Since I had been watching cowboy and Indian movies for years, I knew exactly who Wild Bill and Calamity Jane were. And to think that my grandfather was killed by Indians on a trail drive from Fort Reno,Wyoming, to a point near Devil's Tower, a national monument in Wyoming and his approximate place of death, seemed to put me so close to the old West that I could practically smell the gun smoke.

A little over fifty years later, my wife and I took our son, Matt, back to this area to retrace the steps. That part of South Dakota had not changed much from my first trip. We flew into Rapid City and rented a car to take the Black Hills, Mount Rushmore, Deadwood and Devil's Tower tour. Like I had experienced fifty years earlier, this trip ignited my son's interest in family history. However, this time we decided to find out more when we returned to Houston.

We spent considerable time on the telephone and with the computer over the next six months tracking down family history from any available source. As a result, we put together a booklet on the subject consisting of approximately 250 pages. We turned up a lot of *cousins* we did not about know about. Our research and that of other extended family members over the next couple of years turned up other family history, resulting in a second bound volume of 682 pages.

We found that there were at least eighteen different spellings of the family name. This isn't too difficult to understand when one considers that in the early days there was not a lot of formal education and people often spelled phonetically (and even then sometimes influenced by local dialect).

We now trace the Deffebach (our spelling and that of our *cowboy* ancestor) family as far back as 1560, the date of birth of Michael Diefenbach in Elnhausen, Germany. Michael married Eila Anna in 1590. Michael was a court reporter by trade. The couple had six children, including Martin, who was born in Oberweimar in 1605. Martin was married first to Maria Rubsamen in 1629 and they had six children; she died and he remarried Barbara Romerhauser in 1638, and they produced nine offspring. Martin was a forester for a number of years and was mayor of Nordeck until 1645 and then burger of Marburg. A product of Martin's first marriage was Johann Conrad, born in 1634 in Marburg. Then, Johann Conrad's marriage to Anna Mather in 1658 produced one child in short order, and he was also named Johann Conrad. The second Johann Conrad was married on Christmas day of 1702 to his second wife, Barbara Christler, in Wieslock, a small village founded in 973 on a stream known as the Leimbach, approximately eight miles south of Heidelberg in fruit and wine country.

By way of background, Johann Conrad and his family were part of multitudes of other Germans who were distressed by the hardships following (1) the devastation of war and religious persecution, such as when Louis XIV with the French armies embarked on his policy of religious extermination and (2) the bitter and frightfully cold winter that had descended on Europe in early 1709. William Penn had then recently toured Germany and had been impressed by the work ethics of German farmers and decreed that they would make desirable colonists in Pennsylvania. He had distributed handbills offering large farm lands, laws of their own making, peace and religious freedom to all Christians. Queen Anne of England had German relatives, and she also had distributed pamphlets promising aid and help in migrating to her American colonies. Johann Conrad and his family became part of a mass exodus in late spring of 1709 of approximately ten thousand Germans hoping to relocate to the new land of Pennsylvania in America.

Upon arrival in England, these immigrants created many housing and food problems. Many were housed in temporary quarters in London, but thousands were relocated in Ireland, the Scilly Isles, the West Indies and the Carolinas. Many, who were Catholics and would not renounce their religion, returned to Germany. The English then developed a plan to transport the remainder to New York, not the promised land of Pennsylvania; and they would then be required to pay back the English their immigration costs by extracting tar from the pines trees in the Hudson River area of New York. This commodity was needed by the British navy for shipbuilding. It is estimated that only about one-fourth of the Germans originally migrating to England departed on the eleven ships that sailed to America during the spring and summer of 1710. New York Governor Robert Hunter reported 470 dying in route, with 2,227 arriving in New York City and then continuing up to the Hudson River camp communities. Included was the family of my ancestor, Johann Conrad; and focusing on this point in time, it amazes me that my family arrived in America sixty-six years before the American Revolution and twenty-two years before George Washington, the father of our country, was born.

Moving on, the tar production effort was not successful for a number of reasons; and these remaining German immigrants, who had been working practically as serfs to repay the English, were released by the Governor of New York colony in 1712. Many of these families from the east and west camps on the Hudson, including Johann Conrad's family, relocated to Indian lands at Scholarie. It was here that Johann and Barbara's youngest son, Johann Adam, was born in 1712 as well as their youngest daughter, Dorothea, in 1714. Again transcending numerous hardships and adversities, the Scholarie settlers not only began to prosper, but a core group of thirty-three families (again including my ancestor's family) undertook a remarkable and historic mitigation in 1723 by canoes, rafts and dugouts on the swollen waters of the Susquehanna River to the mouth of the Swatara and then overland to their final destination on the Tulpehocken Creek, in Pennsylvania. At that time, this area was located in the part of Bucks County, which later together with parts of Chester, Lancaster and Philadelphia Counties, became Berks County in 1752.

Johann Conrad's youngest son, Johann Adam, married Sybil Koebel in 1734 and served as a Captain in the French and Indian wars from 1754 through 1763. Four of his sons—Michael, George, Jacob and Peter—served throughout the American Revolutionary War; and my direct ancestor, Michael, was wounded in the Battle of Brandywine Creek fought on September 11, 1777, in Berks County. It was also in 1777 that Johann Adam died; and he is buried in the church cemetery near the stone house he built in Berks County. It is interesting that his son, Jacob, was the first native-born pipe organ builder on this side of the ocean; and he was followed in this craft by his son, grandson and great-grandson. Jacob's first pipe organ is displayed in the Berks County Historical Society Museum.

My ancestor, Michael, was born in 1736 in Tulpehocken, Berks County and married Maria Margaret Anspach. They had six children, including John who was born on October

22, 1781 in Pennsylvania. John married twice: (1) to Maria Margaret Schultz and later (2) to Mary Magdalena Lauer. John had no children by his first wife, but had ten by the second, including my great-great-grandfather, Jeremiah, who was born April 27, 1815 in Berks County. He married Priscilla Catherine Selzer on March 1, 1840 and they had six children, including my great grandfather, John Adam, who was born November 4, 1842.

Jeremiah and his brother William, went West in about 1852 and settled near St. Louis, Missouri, probably at Sullivan. It was Jeremiah and William who shortened their name to Deffebach. Jeremiah's eldest son, John Adam, along with his brothers, Dan and Erasmus "Rassy", were further driven by the pioneer spirit and relocated to the Black Hills area of South Dakota. It was there that they began to systematically supply beef to the mining camps, occasioned by the gold rush to the Black Hills. Dan bought the cattle; John Adam managed the trail drives from Wyoming or wherever purchases of cattle were made; and Rassy sold the cattle and delivered the beef to the mining camps. These brothers (organized much in the same manner as a business organization today with purchasing, sales and transportation departments) established a cattle ranch on the Belle Fourche River, approximately twenty-five miles from Deadwood, South Dakota and north of the present town site of Belle Fourche, South Dakota. It has been said that this was one of the earliest cattle ranches in that part of the country and was later known as the VVV Ranch in modern times.

It was on one of these cattle drives in April of 1880 that John Adam was ambushed and killed by Indians in Wyoming somewhere in the vicinity of the Moorcroft / Sundance / Devil's Tower area. His brother, Dan, and a party of about fifteen other cowboys organized a posse and trailed the Indians for days until they caught up with them near the east prong of the Little Powder River, north and east of the Little Missouri Buttes. The cowboys charged and attacked the Indian camp with vengeance. The Indians disbursed with resulting casualties on both sides according to varying accounts. Many of the horses stolen by the Indians, at the time John Adam was killed, were recovered and not an Indian escaped with a Deffebach horse. Apparently, few of them had any need for one after the cowboys in the posse riddled their camp with bullets.

After John Adam's death, his widowed wife and his children—including my grandfather, Thomas "Tom" George, the second son of John Adam—remained in South Dakota for a time. Tom was graduated in the 1895 class of State Normal Training College in Spearfish. He then ranched for a number of years in the Black Hills area. He had married a classmate, Ethlyn Stephens in 1898; and they had four children, including my father, Lyle, who was born on February 5, 1903. In 1909, Tom moved his family to Texas.

Perhaps, the family movement over the years from the eastern seaboard to the wild and wooly West can best be characterized by Sloan's, "The Pioneers":

A lad looked up at an old, old tree.
At the foot of the mountain peak
And thought of all the stories the tree could tell,
If it could only speak
It stood on the bank by the riverside,
Where the emigrant trail had crossed,
It could tell of the ones that won it through,
Or the ones that had tried and lost.
The West was not won by the timid and weak.
Or the dance hall lady and crook.
Like the old rugged tree standing there all alone,
A man had to have what it took.

A product of so many colorful generations of pioneer stock, it is not surprising that Tom, along with his siblings and children, would also leave a strong legacy of business acumen, church and civic contributions and accomplishments.

Chapter II

EARLY CHILDHOOD

I was born in 1931 in Winters, Texas, which had approximately 1000 inhabitants, mostly of German descent. One of the advantages of growing up in a small town is that you know everybody—the good, the bad and everyone in between. If you wanted to know anything about local gossip, it was easy to find out in those days. All you had to do was to pick up the telephone and you would get *Central*, the local operator; and due to a relatively low volume of telephone traffic, she had plenty of time to listen in on most calls. Consequently, she knew everything going on in town. Also, practically no one could afford a private line because of economic conditions (the Great Depression followed by economic recession); thus, most everybody had a multi-party line. So the locals had plenty to gossip about, if they were so inclined, just by talking to Central and listening to others' conversations on the party line.

We also had our town heroes of a sort. In my eyes, our local Methodist minister, Jimmy Sharbett, was about the most important person. I imagine it was because my parents took me to church with them every time it opened its doors. Accordingly, the exposure to Reverend Sharbett was concentrated, to say the least. When I was only three or four years old, I met his son, Del, when he came to Winters one year to visit his parents. Del was a well-known Mutual Network radio announcer with a deep and powerful voice; and among other things, he gave me a major league baseball autographed by the New York Yankees and an umpire named Ziggy Sears. The ball has disappeared over the years; and that is the only name I can remember. Nonetheless, that was a big deal and promptly played a part in a major decision before me.

It had started with a family friend, who was a rancher doing better than most folks during those recession years. He gave me a goat. I kept it in our back lot behind the back lawn, since, like everyone else in those times, we kept a cow for milk and chickens for eggs. The back lot was also surrounded by a six-foot red picket fence and contained a barn, shed and haystack. The rancher made a *deal* with me that twice a year he would sheer the goat and pay me $1 each time for its wool. Now, I don't know about anyone else, but a buck was really big money in those days. My very first business deal made me feel that someday I could probably lead our country out of its economic quagmire.

It was time to name my goat while Del was in town for his visit; and after Sunday church services, both Del and his father each asked me to name my goat after them. They feigned great concern between themselves that each name was more suitable than the other one's for such a valuable pet. They had obviously heard of my shrew business deal with the rancher, who was also a member of the congregation. I had to choose and was in a tight spot. Besides being grateful to Del for the baseball, I was impressed with his national reputation. He was constantly on the airwaves and of course, radio and newspaper were the only media games in the country at that time.

After due deliberation and soul searching, I announced after church the following Sunday (Del's last day in town) the name of my goat was *Jimmy*. Even if our minister was not as famous as his son, he had asked me to name it after him and I felt this was the right thing to do. He had always and continuously been in my life. The minister made a big deal of the *recognition*. Del was also very gracious and told me he understood my decision, since he also had great respect for his father.

With this big decision out of the way, life with Jimmy began on a day-to-day basis. I soon learned that Jimmy was extremely smart. I could *sic* him on any of the neighborhood bullies, and he would tree them and sit under the tree guarding his prey all day or until I called him off. My respect in the neighborhood was greatly enhanced. Jimmy also quickly learned to play *hide-and-seek* with the rest of the kids. As one may or may not remember, one player would be *it* and he or she would close their eyes for an agreed-upon count and then come looking for the other players who were hiding. The first person found would then become the next *it.* Jimmy was good at hiding. He first tried to hide behind the haystack but soon found he could burrow into the haystack itself and really conceal himself quite well. Next, Jimmy learned how to be *it,* even though he was seldom the first found. He may or may not have closed his eyes or actually counted in the barn, where our local rules required *it* to go for the agreed count, but he would wait in the barn long enough for everyone to hide. He excelled in finding everyone no matter whether they chose to hide in or behind the barn, shed, haystack or elsewhere on the lot. I cannot speak about goats in general, but this one was one *smart hombre.* Besides, over the next year he endured two sheerings by our rancher friend, making him highly productive for my otherwise meager budget. This prosperity was short lived. About this time, my dad had finally saved enough money to replace his relic of a car with a newer model that still had shiny paint. During these tough times, one can imagine what an event and morale booster this car was to my parents. Then one Sunday morning, the car was parked in the driveway and had been freshly washed. We were preparing for church services, and I happened to walk to the back door to wave to Jimmy in the fenced-in back lot. Just as I looked out of the door, I saw Jimmy hurdle the six foot picket fence. I had never known him to do that before.

He immediately ran to the driveway, apparently to see the shiny bright car. It was so shiny you could see your face in it. He did. Instantly, he decided that there was another goat trespassing on this territory. Quick as lightning, he decided to dispatch the trespasser. He took a running leap and rammed the goat's likeness reflected on the car door with the fury of his mighty horns. Jimmy was proud of his accomplishment. After all, the other goat had gone away and only crumpled metal remained. But my dad was livid, and my worst fears were realized that afternoon when our rancher friend picked up Jimmy to return him to his ranch. I had a lot of neighborhood friends, many of whom I would have gladly sacrificed in Jimmy's place, but that was not an option. That day, I lost the best friend I had ever had and who could never be replaced. I never saw Jimmy again, but the rancher gave me periodic reports that he was living well, had married and raised a number of kids. Since the rancher also attended our church, I figured he would not lie.

Having lost my clout in the neighborhood with Jimmy gone, it wasn't long until the largest bully in the neighborhood started coming over regularly to devil me. After all, he now had more time since he didn't have to spend so much of it in a tree. I had a sandbox in the back yard, equipped with a small bucket, rake and shovel. The kid delighted in taking away from me whatever I was playing with in the sandbox and then playing with it himself. This went on for some time.

One day my dad came home from work to have lunch at home. He witnessed what was going on, and that night he took me aside and told me that I was going to have to learn to take up for myself. He said everyone eventually had to learn to defend their interests and property from those who would otherwise take it from them. He wasn't very specific about how I should do this, but I gathered the gist was that I should become physical, if necessary, to protect my soil. Within the next day or so, I had my chance to do so. The bully came and promptly took a little shovel away from me and commenced to dig. I assessed the situation in the light of my dad's conversation and decided to defend my dignity and property by whacking the kid with my small rake. The first blow was on the top of his head and it made a sizeable cut on his scalp. Blood gushed and the boy ran home screaming bloody murder.

Fortunately, the injury was not as serious as it looked. But I couldn't wait until my dad came home that night to let him know that I had done exactly what he had told me to do by standing up for myself. Somehow, I got the idea that he wasn't overly excited about the outcome, particularly since the kid's parents were fairly close friends. After the incident blew over, my dad had other conversations with me about self-defense. The point of these later discussions seemed to be about moderation and reasonable response in light of the type of risk posed. As far as I was concerned, the big thing about the whole ordeal was that this kid and I never had any more trouble and became fast friends for the rest of the time I lived in Winters.

Vacation time was always a wonderful experience in these hard economic times. I say wonderful because vacations like games were usually invented and/or improvised in those days. In our case, my dad took an ordinary pull trailer with a flatbed as a platform. On it, he constructed what I will loosely call a recreational vehicle. Nothing like we know them today, but a very inexpensive and workable trailer to pull behind the car on trips. In the early days, we would use it to camp out on the Llano River near Junction, Texas. The trailer was equipped with two feet of drawer space immediately above the trailer platform, which would hold essentials like cooking utensils, plates and flatware. The drawers also housed food and like provisions, as well as some wash rags, towels and a change of bed sheets. The latter was due to the fact that just above the drawer space, there was a horizontal platform on which there was a mattress. There was also enough headspace so that my parents could sleep in this makeshift bed with the trailer roof above them and usually the doors on the side open, covered with mosquito netting. It looked quite comfortable, but I had to sleep in the car as the mattress, probably twin size, would not hold more than my dad and mom.

We would set out trout lines to catch fish at night, and then we fished from the banks during the day. There were a lot of fish in the Llano in those days, and we were usually very lucky to catch some fairly decent cat fish on the trout line, and then catch some bass, perch and more catfish during the day. We would clean them promptly and ice them down in a sort of a cooler, but not as efficient as today's *Igloo* coolers. Of course, the best part was eating the fish while they were so fresh.

For several years, I had a cat named *Whiteman*. Needless to say the cat was predominately white. He loved climbing all the big oaks along the river bank. This went on for several years; and each year when we got the trailer out of the barn, Whiteman was the first to sense it was time for adventure. This worked well until on one trip time it rained and rained, flooding the river. We had to pack to evacuate as quickly as possible, as the river was rapidly rising. I panicked as we were about ready to leave to return home. I could not find Whiteman. We called and looked as long as we could, but could not find him anywhere. We had no choice but to leave the swollen river area.

That was the last time I saw Whiteman, and I was very disappointed. I have to confess, however, I never did like cats as much as goats. We made one more trip to the Llano when I was in the first grade, but did not run across him. We had found out, in the meantime, by talking with some of the people who lived in the area that he had survived the flood and was often seen along the river. This information made me feel better, even though he had decided that he could do quite well without us.

On this last trip to the Llano, I involuntarily learned to swim. My dad and mother had been trying to get me to learn on each vacation trip. Somehow, it had not appealed to me to swim in the river when you could not see anything around you in the murky water. I never learned at home, because I do not believe that there was a single swimming pool in Winters. Anyway, my dad had enough of my resistance about swimming; he scooped me up one day and threw me into the Llano near our campsite. I surfaced and fortunately found a large rock underneath me on which to stand. Dad was yelling at me from the bank to swim to him. I told him I did not know how to swim. That was true at the moment I said it, but about that time, I looked behind me at the opposite bank of the river in time to see a cotton-mouthed water moccasin push off the bank. He was coming right at me, and I was a good twenty feet from shore. More by reflex than conscious action, I immediately *swam* to shore where my dad was now panicked, having seen the snake moving toward me. I have swum a thousand times since, but I believe my first swim in the Llano River was my fastest time. At any rate, my dad was glad I made it safely to shore and learned to swim at the same time.

After completing the first grade, our family moved to a larger town: Sweetwater, Texas. It must have had a population of at least four thousand to five thousand people in 1938 when we moved there. I was apprehensive about the first day of school as I started second grade. I did not know a soul at that time. I quickly found out that Sweetwater had its share of bullies too. My first day at school was greeted by considerable harassment, pushing and shoving as some type of apparent welcome for any new kid coming to town. I had no idea how long this miserable treatment would go on, so on impulse I decided to have it out with the bully ringleader the first day.

We squared off, and I did my best to remember all of my dad's previous advice on reasonable response and so on. Instead of any physical assistance such as a rake or other equalizer, I landed a few punches early, as did he; but I was able to wrestle him to the ground and finally pin him down. This was enough to cause him and the other bullies to back off. This was the day that I realized most bullies are cowards and never expect their prey to fight back. I didn't physically whip this bigger, older boy. I simply did the unexpected and caught him off guard, carried the fight to him and he didn't have the heart or guts to chance the uncertainty of what might happen to embarrass him among his peers. This brought the encounter to a quick conclusion. The test was over and I had no more problems at that school. For me, it was a lesson well learned for the future.

It wasn't long until I met the guy my age across the street from our house, and he turned out not only to be a good friend, but a valuable one to know. His parents owned the town's only bakery. Many a Saturday morning, he would take me to the bakery which was *downtown* and was in walking distance of our houses. We would eat our fill of freshly baked bread, cookies and the like before spending our dime allowances by going to one of the town's two movie houses around the corner on the town's square for the afternoon matinee—always cowboys and Indians, of course.

My only concern with this friendship had to do with his big sister, *Tootsie*. She was several years older than us and was known for her temper and particularly the intolerance for her brother's intrusion into her space in their house. My worst experience was witnessing an outburst one day when we were playing in his house and were making considerable noise for some reason I have long since forgotten. She came out of her room armed with a pair of scissors and appeared out of control. We didn't take any chances and immediately ran to the front door to escape outside. She threw the scissors in our direction as we were leaving, and I will never forget seeing those scissors sticking in the door above our heads as we flew through it to safety. I never even asked whether she really intended to do that or whether the scissors accidentally left her wildly waving hand. I think I was afraid to ask. In any event, we usually played at or around my house after that enlightening experience.

It turned out that the problem didn't last very long, since my dad decided to move on after I finished the second grade to take advantage of an offer to purchase his own insurance agency in nearby Snyder, Texas; and at the same time, to become a partner in a local public accounting firm there. This was 1939; the recession was continuing and he felt this was a career opportunity that might not repeat. Anyway, I now knew how to handle the first day at a new school. I also had developed some doubts about the importance of Sweetwater, because all I ever heard about its importance from others is that *all the girls bathed in Sweetwater and dressed in Plainview.* The latter being a reference to another small West Texas town. I was not entirely sure if I understood that reference since I was only eight, but it didn't sound like the two towns could be very much if folks didn't remember them for anything but a place to bath and dress.

Chapter III

MY HOMETOWN

I have always considered Snyder, Texas, as my *home town* and where I am *from*. For a small town, it had a good school system, consisting of one location, a main building with three wings, containing elementary, junior high and high schools. Additionally, there was an auditorium in the center of the three wings and a separate gymnasium building on the same piece of property. Several blocks away the Texas Friday Night Special (otherwise known as the football field) occupied its own space.

The fact that Snyder had a good school system is not related to the physical plant, but rather to the quality of its teachers and administrators. Like with businesses, sticks and stones are not as important as its people. For example, Mrs. Hornsby taught all subjects in the one and only third-grade class. She instilled in me a desire to learn and compete both in and out of the classroom. My memory is not entirely clear as to her precise teaching style and methods, but I am sure it was basic, involving the blackboard, flash cards, ovals and slashes, memorizing, a short nap and plenty of discipline. I always thought of her as my education foundation. I had not developed any such a feeling about school in the first and second grades in Winters and Sweetwater. In a geography lesson one day she made the statement that if Russia ever awoke, it would be a super power in the world. That did not rock my world at the time (1939-40), but I thought about it a number of times after her *prediction* came to pass.

After Mrs. Hornsby's fine tuning, I never had much trouble in school. I was not seriously challenged thereafter in studies, at least until I came face-to-face with Pop Patterson, who taught chemistry, Algebra I and II in high school. He was one tough coot. I nearly burned down the school during a chemistry experiment, but somehow managed to survive the course. But Pop was really tough in algebra. He had some type of sadistic side that caused him to make many of the answers to his test questions come out in fractions. The answer never did look or feel right. Moreover, after a few fractional answers in a sequence during a test, you were also uncomfortable with a subsequent answer that came out with even numbers. The bottom line was that Pop gave me such a sound foundation in high school algebra that I received A+ in both Algebra I and II in college. Thanks to all the good teachers like Hornsby and Patterson, and setting aside modesty entirely, I finished first in my graduating classes in elementary and junior high schools and second in my high school graduating class. My story on the latter is that a girl transferred to our senior class from a nearby community and was permitted to transfer her grades as well. Smart as she was, I think she would have still been first if she had attended Snyder High School the entire time. But at least, it gave me an excuse for dropping the academic ball, so to speak.

My hometown also offered additional exposures to a well-rounded upbringing. There was 100 percent cooperation between parents, schools and the churches in this small West Texas town. For example, in a history class taught by Ms. Jones, a long tall drink of water, I inadvertently missed my target with a spitball while Ms. Jones was turned toward the blackboard writing an assignment. On this luckless day, it landed squarely on her lanky behind with the explosive force of a scud missile. Lacking a reputation for bad conduct at school, I can only presume that I looked so guilty that she did not even ask who did it. Instead, she reached for her baseball-bat-sized paddle and beckoned me to come outside into the hall. She shut the door and then damaged my backside to a far greater extent than the injury I accidentally inflicted on her. We returned to the classroom. She calmly sat down and I relaxed somewhat at the apparent armistice. However, while still at her desk and before returning to complete the assignment on the blackboard, she called me forward once again and handed me a folded note to take to the school principal. I did and after reading it, he took out his surf-board-sized paddle and blackened all the areas Ms. Jones had left undone during her unrestrained violence to my body part that goes out of doors last.

I was really glad when the last bell of the day rang, and I limped home. A footnote is that at our school practically no mother picked up their kids in a car. Most families didn't have but one anyway and the dads used it in their work. Everyone walked or rode a bicycle home even in high school and regardless of the elements. I still shudder when I think of Memorial High School in Houston where some of our kids attended school. The big problem they had was where to park all the students' BMWs. But back to the subject at hand, although my hand was not the part of my anatomy that was in issue, my mother met me at the door and had heard all about her prodigal son's day at school, in which he had highlighted and enlivened the day's otherwise serene activities. Her weapon of choice was always the same. She had me go out to the backyard and cut a healthy switch off a tree. She reserved the right to reject any offering which she didn't feel was sturdy enough to do a good job. On this occasion, she did a good job. I was so numb when my dad got home later that evening, I just assumed the usual position and let him whack away with his rattlesnake skin belt. Thereafter, the word *spitball*, whether launched by hand or rubber band, was not even in my vocabulary. The amazing part of this yarn is how word traveled from school or church or anywhere else in town where misbehavior was witnessed. It was so organized that even the lady, who owned the only movie house in town and manned the ticket window, would call our parents to tattle after taking our money when we committed the cardinal sin of going to the movies on Sunday afternoon between the short hiatus between Sunday morning service and the evening service. The same type of informational pipeline was present if we attended any type of public dance. The good news, as a corollary to this saga, is that I have never ever heard of any of my contemporaries, who grew up in this conspiratorial atmosphere, doing dope or getting in trouble with the law.

Another activity that was very beneficial in developing values that could guide one along life's path was scouting. My mother organized a Cub Scout pack early on in Snyder. She was the den mother and all of our meetings were at our house. Our pack probably had about fifteen kids. It was a lot of fun and good preparatory training for the Boy Scouts. Projects were always interesting and we all loved to advance to a higher rank, such as from Bobcat to Wolf, Wolf to Bear and so on. Looking back, it seems that everything required to advance to higher ranks was designed to develop character and promote good citizenship. When we were twelve years old, most of us joined the Boy Scouts. Once again, this was great adventure and fun for the boys of our small community. We were exposed to valuable moral and ethical values along scouting's trail. My dad was also involved in scouting and was the president of the Buffalo Trail Council which was headquartered in Midland, Texas. I do recall that about the time I obtained Eagle Scout status, he trumped me and received the Silver Beaver award for his outstanding service to scouting. However, he was as proud of me as I was of him. There are at least two things I do not think I will ever forget—my USMC serial number and the Boy Scout pledge: "On my honor, I will do my best to do my duty to God and my country and to obey the Scout law; to help other people at all times; to keep myself physically strong, mentally awake and morally straight." It is difficult to chart a much better course to travel through teenage years and even beyond.

One of the biggest thrills every summer was going to Philmont Scout Ranch in southern New Mexico near Cimarron. This was a camp out facility in my day, although I have heard that they have some fine facilities today. We slept in tents in the rugged wilderness of about two hundred acres. We backpacked into the mountains and along the trails. On many occasions, we would skinny dip in the cold mountain streams. Fun was had by all, and we usually earned several merit badges at camp. The trip *to and from* was as much fun as camp. All of our scouts, as well as some in smaller towns around Snyder, were transported to and from Philmont in an open cattle truck. Can you imagine anyone having this experience today? It was great fun and very exciting. We made several stops along the way, and our favorite game was to draw a crowd around the truck and then our driver lifted the back end of the cattle trailer up several feet with all of us in it. The locals would *oh and ah* and almost always applaud for him. He was super strong and was a deaf mute. But none of us had any trouble communicating with him by improvised sign language and he was truly our hero. Equally important, he was annually the driver on every trip that we made to Philmont. I cannot truthfully say that our annual excursion would have been as much fun without him.

The other type of activity that influenced my teen years was the participation in all high school sports. Of course, football was king. In fact, we played basketball, baseball, tennis and track the rest of the school year just to stay in shape for football. We had the delusion that we could win the state football championship in our classification our senior year. This was real enough to us that our coach talked most of us in joining the Texas National Guard so that we would not be drafted out of high school. Everyone viewed this as a real risk as we commenced our sophomore year in 1945 before the end of World War II. The sad truth is that, although we won most of our games in our senior year, we didn't even advance to the playoffs as we lost our last regular season game to Roscoe 6-0. In a way, it was not a disgrace to lose to them, because their school allowed their senior players to flunk a course and stay over from year to year to play ball. I remember seeing them get off their school bus before our game. They did their best to intimidate our *kids*(whom our principal would never let stay over by flunking a course to play football), having all grown beards for the game, most wearing six-year letter stripes on their football jackets and some of them bringing their wives and kids to the game. The guy that I had to block had a name something like *Thor*, weighed 340 pounds and went on to become an All Southwest Conference tackle. I was 6 feet 3 inches tall and weighed 152 pounds and felt like chopped meat after that game. I would be amiss not to mention that I played center on offense and in the backfield on defense. I wasn't extremely talented, but small towns in those days were lucky to field twenty-two or more players. Anyway, I like to brag that my substitute was Grant Teaff, who went on to football fame as a player, coach and motivational speaker. Most sports fans will recall that he coached at Baylor for many years and then went on to league administration. Sometimes I forget on days that start with a "T" (like Tuesday, Thursday and sometimes on Taturday and Tunday) to mention that I was a senior when Grant was a freshman substitute at center.

Although times were not easy toward the end of the recession and the initial days of World War II, it was not difficult to find jobs to make money if you really wanted to work. From the time we first moved to Snyder until I went to college, I had a morning job that did not produce cash, but did help my dad make ends meet. I was the janitor of the second floor of the two-story downtown building where my dad's office was located, along with his accounting partnership and a local real estate office with which he had some affiliation. I would get up at about 4:30 AM., dress and brush my hair and teeth but not necessarily with the same brush. I would then ride my bike downtown, sweep and dust the second floor as well as the stairway from there to the ground entrance. I would then ride my bike home, eat breakfast and then ride my bike to school.

On Saturdays and during the summer months, I had a variety of jobs around town. In the war years, I worked for the Pick & Pay grocery store. My classmate's parents owned the store, and her dad was overseas with the Navy. Her mother ran the store in his absence, and my classmate, Sandra Josephson, and I worked part time to help out on the store's busiest day, Saturday. We kept the store clean, carried out groceries for the customers and did other odd jobs. Sometimes when we were not too busy, we hung out in the back portion of the store where the feed sacks were stored. We also learned all the codes for stuff that was hard to get during the war years. A *pound of forty-two* referred to a pound of bacon priced at 42 cents per pound. *One hundred forty-nine* meant a pair of silk hose priced at $1.49. The *brown one* referred to a Hershey bar. Not even the wind talkers could crack this code. At the age of fourteen with the consent of my parents and the approval of the County Judge, I obtained a driver's license. I was then promoted to delivery boy, making runs in the store's ancient pickup truck. It was painted bright orange and could be seen from miles away. This was really a good job, and I stayed with it until Sandra's dad returned from the service.

I worked for several other retail establishments on Saturdays after retiring from Pick & Pay. I did not last too long at the local J. C. Penny store, as selling shirts and underwear was boring compared to delivering groceries. I did better at helping out at the local soda fountain where the fringe benefits were good. I also formed a business partnership with Jack Gorman, and we cut grass for our neighbors. This was good business. We also used some of the profits to buy a paint gun, and then we solicited everyone we knew to paint their cars. The only taker we got was my granddad who let us paint his 1936 Chevrolet. It didn't look too bad, except for a few places in which the black paint had been generously applied with resulting *runs* down the sides. My granddad was a good sport, but we were not able to expand this sideline business venture because in a small town, everyone knew who had painted his car. Our best money was made during cotton picking season. The work was hard, but we got paid daily based on the weight of the sacks of cotton bolls we had pulled that day. Besides the money being reasonably good, you always got a good night's sleep because this seasonal work was hard and hot, and we were exhausted at the end of the day. A fringe benefit was that we reported for football season in reasonably good shape.

When we were not working and sometimes on Sunday afternoons, we had another diversion within walking distance of our homes, which at the time were near the south city limits of Snyder. Just outside of town there were a number of fenced areas containing various types of livestock. We liked to visit one in particular where the star attraction was an albino mule we called *Speedy Butler*. On these visits, we would have a minirodeo of sorts. Our gang would take turns riding Speedy, or attempting to, and the winner was whoever could stay aboard the longest. Speedy did one of the best imitations of a bull ride I ever saw, and he had it in his head that no one could ride bareback on him for long. He would buck, kick and sometimes even roll over, but he always won one way or the other. One of the *other* tricks in his book (and it the most dangerous for the rider) was to run under a branch of one of the many mesquite trees on his place. I have no clue as to how he did it, but he would choose a branch that on the dead run would clear his back by only several inches. The rider had two options: *Option A* was to jump off Speedy's back before the branch hit you in the chest or belly; or *Option B* the branch would hit you in the chest or belly. Normally, this was Speedy's last resort to dispose of the unwanted rider, as he would far rather buck you off. From this description, one can see why the winner was decided by total ride time rather prevailing over the will of Speedy by riding him until he stopped. Of course, the latter was never going to happen. Except on the occasion of a busted rib or two, this was always great fun and certainly was more thrilling than most of our free-time activities.

I only can remember one other great peril in growing up in Snyder. That involved two of our senior citizens. One was my grandfather, Tom, and the other was a retired minister, Brother Clark. They each had black 1936 model cars, one a Chevrolet and the other a Pontiac. However, they were virtually identical in appearance. If any local saw what appeared to be either one of them driving near an intersection, he or she had to be sure which senior citizen they were observing. What made this imperative was that my grandfather stopped at every intersection, whether or not there were any stop signs or traffic lights. On the other hand, Brother Clark never stopped at any intersection, regardless of the presence or absence of stop signs or traffic lights. Since your life might depend upon automobile recognition, most of the local folks would just stop or otherwise get out of the intersection area until the observed vehicle passed rather than guess at the occupant's identity.

Other than this traffic problem, Snyder was a great hometown; and even today, it is a good place to be *from*. I think often of our neighborhood gang. Jack Gorman was the most handsome, and he played quarterback on our football team. Robert Pruitt was our runt, but tough as nails. He was by far the best marbles shooter. He was nominated, accepted, and graduated from the United States Military Academy. Unfortunately, he passed at a rather early age. When we first moved to Snyder, housing was scare and we rented the upstairs of John Sentell's house. He was being recalled as a colonel in the army as things were heating up in Europe just before World War II. His sons, Marvin and Joe, were part of our neighborhood group. Marvin played football with us, but Joe was not too healthy for a few years during this time. He and Marvin, his older brother, had been playing with his dad's military .45-caliber pistol, as his dad was preparing to go back into the army; and Marvin had accidentally shot Joe in the spleen. Fortunately, there was no permanent damage but it did leave Joe somewhat underdeveloped for a while. Donnie Everett was a running back on our football team and a crack shot with a BB gun. I had an indentation on my forehead for some time as proof of that statement. He was as close as we had to a *cowboy* in our gang as his parents had a ranch. So did Mark McLaughlin's parents. He didn't go to Snyder High School but attended and graduated from Culver Military Academy. However, during the summer months he hung out with us and we had many hunting expeditions on his parents' ranch. As near as I ever came to being killed was on one of those occasions.

We were hunting jack rabbits from the back of his pickup cross country; that is, we were driving across fields without roads of any type, scaring up rabbits and shooting them, or at least at them, from the open pickup bed. Mark was driving and it was my turn to shoot. A rabbit jumped up and the chase was on. Mark had to turn the pickup to the right sharply, and I was shooting from the left side of it. The pickup made the turn; and I did not, rolling over and over wrapped around my .22-caliber rifle. I thought I was dead because when I first regained consciousness, I could not breathe. I didn't see angels; however, I could then see everyone from the pickup running towards me. Then I started breathing again because the fall had literally knocked the wind out of me. We continued hunting, and it was not until that evening when we went to town to bowl that I realized that there were other injuries from the fall. I attempted to pick up a bowling ball with my left hand supporting it and the ball fell to the floor. Subsequent X-rays revealed three of the small bones in my left hand were broken. Sometimes it seemed if I didn't have bad luck, I wouldn't have had any luck at all. Football season was approaching, and as it turned out, I had to play the first three or four games with a cast on my left hand that extended to my elbow. Somehow, it accidentally wound up in the opposing players' faces or other body parts now and then, and I wasn't very popular in some of the towns in our district that year.

Our gang had an additional member from across town. This was Gerald Heinzelmann, aka *Heine* or *Jerry*. In Snyder, being from across town was no handicap in playing with our gang, since if you were driving through Snyder, you couldn't blink or you might be out of town. Jerry spent some time in the military; then I lost track of him but recently learned he owns the local hardware store in Cloudcroft, New Mexico. As of this writing, he and his wife, Carolyn, are still there. There was one other person in our neighborhood who participated in some of our activities we improvised to kill time. She was Anne McMullin, who lived with her parents in our immediate neighborhood. Parents and other neighbors often thought we were too tough with Anne in contact games and the like, but the truth of the matter was she could whip any one of us and she knew it. This put her in sort of an associate membership status, since it just didn't seem right in those days to have a full-fledged female member of your neighborhood gang who could throw you three out of four falls.

The bottom line is we all grew up together, played together, worked together, most participated in sports together, scouted together and four of us later ended up rooming together in our junior year in college. More will be said about that later. In looking back over all the years that have intervened since that time, the advantages of what we learned from church, school, good parenting, good friends and general small-town philosophy are obvious to me. There is also lifetime value in the lessons learned from scouting and sports: *teamwork*, *leadership* and *common sense improvising*. All forms of education, formal or self-taught through reading or experience have great value in dealing with the uncertainties and opportunities of life. But one's greatest asset, other than good health and a belief in God, is *common sense*. Without it, education is often wasted. I say this based on what I have learned over the years from observing and listening to some *overeducated idiots* I have known. I define an *overeducated idiot* as one who has all the advantages of formal education; but has failed to accomplish his potential because either he was behind the door when God handed out *common sense* or fell so in love with himself and academic accomplishments along the way that he lost it.

Chapter IV

DESTINATION COLLEGE

In the fall of 1948, I made the long journey from Snyder to Abilene, Texas (about eighty miles down the road) to commence my dad's carefully orchestrated plans for my college education. It was to commence by attending McMurry College, which at the time was the smallest of Abilene's three church colleges with a student body of about eight hundred students. My dad reasoned that it was best for a small-town boy to have a small college transition from high school before moving on to a large university to obtain a bachelor of business administration with a major in public accountancy, That target was the University of Texas with a student body at that time of some twenty-five thousand students. Not only had he predetermined the schools I would attend, but he had catalogs from both institutions and had the curriculum laid out semester after semester for the entire four years. To say that he had given some thought to my college education would be a drastic understatement. For in addition to an undergraduate degree, he also felt that it would be necessary to obtain a law degree, in order to protect the accounting degree from lawyers. He was sure that they intended to take away the accountant's ability to handle federal tax matters and file income tax returns. Hindsight tells me that this was an unreasonable fear in that most of the lawyers I know have not had any desire to deal with the complications of federal tax law or the drudgery of preparing tax returns.

His selection of McMurry was also driven in part by the fact that I had been offered scholastic and basketball scholarships at that school. Fortunately, the scholastic scholarship was not conditional; since during the first week of basketball practice, I tore the cartilage in my right knee and was not be able to participate my freshman year. Moreover, since I would be at the school for only two years, it was not likely I could get a scholarship for one year only. As fate would have it, this was little more than idle speculation, as McMurry turned out to have an unusually good basketball team those two years; and I do not think they would have had much need for me.

When I arrived at McMurry, there was only one car on campus, and it belonged to a Bible student who had been given the car, about a 1931 Pierce Arrow, by an elderly woman he had met back east when he was selling Bibles the previous summer. Some may remember this make of car. It had two spare tires mounted on each side of the car in the front fenders just in forward of the door and the headlights were enormous chrome objects. That student owner couldn't afford to drive this beast as it broke down easily and knew how to gulp gas before the words *gas guzzler* were even coined. But its owner was not stupid. Since the car had pull down blinds inside the windows, he would rent it by the hour to fellow students on the weekends and evenings for spooning. It was really the only privacy afforded anywhere on this church controlled campus. Additionally, these were the days some schools put *saltpeter* in the food in an effort to help control raging hormones. Even so, it was the most popular spot on the campus. Why the faculty didn't exorcize it from the campus, I will never know.

In any event, it became apparent that to be anybody on the campus, it would be handy to have a car. I immediately started a campaign with my parents for one, but they resisted until the second semester of my freshman year. They finally told me to pick out one from a used car lot in Abilene for $50 or less. This was not an easy challenge, but I went looking anyway. Much to my surprise, I found a beauty; and when the salesman asked how much I could spend on it, I told him $50. He said that was the exact price of this car, a 1938 Willys coupe. Of course, its black paint was somewhat faded and the grey upholstery was torn in a number of places.

I didn't realize it had other deficiencies until I drove it home to Snyder the next weekend. I quickly found out that it used as much oil as it did gasoline. My dad was somewhat disillusioned about my due diligence in buying a used car. Anyhow, I convinced him that it was better than my hitchhiking eighty miles back and forth from school to home on weekends, which my roommate and I had done on several occasions. But by the time we got home, it was about time to hook it up and go back. This logic swayed him. He then suggested that I contact my uncles, Vernon and Arthur, who owned a garage in Ranger, Texas, and get an estimate for a rebuilt engine. I did this, and over the next several months they completely reworked this jewel mechanically for about $250. *We* now had $300 invested. It drove so good, got excellent gas mileage and didn't seem to use a drop of oil. Therefore, it occurred to me that something should be done to the exterior paint and interior trim to bring them up to par with this cool smooth running engine. I resumed negotiations with my dad, since it had been *his* idea to fix up the engine. After somewhat lengthy negotiations, he told me to go to a local paint shop in Abilene and get an estimate. I did this very promptly so that this project wouldn't interfere with my studies. I got an estimate to repaint this very small car and completely reupholster it, including a new head liner, for $200. I convinced my dad that if *we* sprang for this, we still would only have a $500 investment in this really spiffy car worthy of a straight-A student, who then would not then have to worry about its condition to the point of letting a B or so slip in somewhere unexpectedly. Again, logic prevailed. He didn't even ask about my color scheme, which was green metallic paint outside and red leather inside, including a red headliner.

When this baby came out of the shop, it was clear that it was the finest car in Abilene, well at least on our campus. As a matter of fact, when I had completed the first year at McMurry, the local Snyder Jeep dealer offered to trade me even for a new 1949 Jeep Wagoneer. After a lot of thought, I swapped with him, but for years I missed the green metallic bug. I also traded the Jeep for a 1949 Plymouth before leaving McMurry.

My roommate was Hollis Robison from Sweetwater, Texas. I did not know him when we lived in Sweetwater, but over the next two years we became very close. One of our suitemates was named Bartel LaRue. He was a standup comedian. For years, I fully expected to see him listed on the screen credits of some of the slap stick comic movie. I never did and do not know whatever happened to him after school. Hollis and I had many good times at McMurry. He later went to law school at St. Mary's in San Antonio, and I next saw him when we were taking the bar exam. We were able to have lunch and/or dinner together during the three-day bar sessions. He and some of his classmates about convinced me that I had failed each session when they kicked around the questions asked each morning or afternoon session and their answers. St Mary's directed its course studies to passing the bar; and these students said that all the answers could be found in actual Texas cases, often using the name of those cases in their post mortem discussions, i.e., Blank vs. Blank, Jones vs. Somebody and the like. UT law school, when I attended, didn't teach much Texas law; instead, they taught you how to think and reason in grey areas. Later I learned that the answers to most legal problems in litigation are seldom black and white. The faculties of Texas, Harvard, Yale and the other great law schools, who teach the same way, are noted for the success of their graduates. A footnote to what will come later is that I passed the bar exam, but several of Hollis's classmates who had scared me to death did not. I never saw Hollis thereafter, but I talked to him on one occasion when he was in the district attorney's office in San

Antonio. Someone told me later on that Hollis had passed, but I was never able to confirm that.

Having gotten to know most of the basketball players during my limited time with the team, I did have the good fortune to develop some friendships with some team members, as well as other athletes who participated in other sports and lived in the athletic dorm. One of the best was the star running back for McMurry, Brad Rowland. Brad was from Hamlin, Texas, and I played against him for two years in high school. He was outstanding then; however, Hamlin did not have many other good players to compliment him and he could not reach his maximum potential at that time. Of all the college football players I have observed over the years, I know of only two or three that I felt were as good as or better than Brad. He was the type of running back who could plough through a good defensive line, but also had the speed to run around the ends. He was not known as a *speedster* as such, but he could usually run as fast as *he had to*. He also had many moves he could put on the defensive backfield. As a result of his heroics and the rest of McMurry's very sound first and second teams, McMurry won practically all of its games over the two-year period I was in attendance there. The small school powerhouse, by reputation, in those days was the Missouri Valley Vikings. McMurry played them both years in the Oleander Bowl in Galveston and won both games. In one of them, I will never forget a good example of Brad's diversity. He took a direct high snap from center on third and long with the line of scrimmage being about his own twenty-yard line. He raced toward the sideline on his right, but the delay from recovering the high snap prevented him from being able to get around the mob of Missouri Valley defenders converging on him. So Brad quick kicked the ball on the run and it sailed over eighty yards and came to rest on the Viking's one foot line. If he had run out of bounds or been tackled, it would have been fourth down; and McMurry's punter would have been lucky to get it out to the fifty-yard line.

Brad also had other talents. He played a wicked piano by ear, and the girls found this equally exciting as watching him on the football field. There were certain advantages in being Brad's friend and hanging out with him. He was also a very good golfer. Just as soon as football season was over, we would head to the links. He played golf left handed, and on his first outing of the year, it would not be unusual for him to shoot in the low seventies. I happened to play golf left handed in those days too, but I was not a natural *lefty* nor nearly as good as Brad. I had started playing golf on the sand greens on a rundown nine-hole golf course in Winters. My dad and his partners in the banking business would sometimes play golf after work if light conditions permitted. I tagged along when I could, since I have always loved to play. My dad played left handed, although he was right handed at all other things. The golf club shafts were wooden in those days, and the three golf clubs I had (a wood of some type, an iron and a putter) were old clubs of his that he cut down for me. By the time I was playing with Brad, I had a full set of clubs but seldom was able to beat him. Nevertheless, we had a lot of fun playing the somewhat rugged and less than fully maintained golf courses of West Texas.

Brad went on to make first team Little All-American in both his junior and senior years. I do not remember anyone else doing this but Eddie LeBarron. As a side light, I also played golf with Eddie during an NFL quarterback amateur event sponsored by General Motors some years ago at Lake Walden near Conroe, Texas. He, like Brad, was also a very good golfer off season. Brad played for the Chicago Bears but did not have an extended career as he was drafted during the Korean conflict. After discharge, he went to work for Anderson Clayton in Atlanta.

Another good friend at McMurry was a guard who was from my hometown, Raymond Bynum. I played one year at Snyder with him and then several more with his younger brother, Don, who also went to McMurry. I was Don's best man when he married in his sophomore year, and I think he would agree that with a best man like me, he didn't need any enemies. When he and his bride were getting into their getaway honeymoon car, I closed the car door on his fingers. Don informed me upon his return from a short honeymoon, that his throbbing fingers prevented the honeymoon trip from being all he had anticipated. To make a long story short, he finally forgave me before I left McMurry for UT.

I previously mentioned that our football coach in high school had us participate in all other sports, including basketball, just to keep in shape for football. I later learned that this was not the case in all parts of the country. Dick Ritchie, another good friend that I met at McMurry was a basketball player from Lebanon, Indiana. Our basketball coach at McMurry did a lot of recruiting in Indiana, and three members of our first team were from there. One year during the Christmas holidays I went home with them and everywhere in Lebanon, basketball was the main topic for discussion. One reason was at that time, there were no high school divisions in Indiana for basketball based upon the size of the school or town. Any team could compete for the state championship. And the state champion was indeed the best team in the state, regardless of school or town population. Basketball was king. In fact, many of the smaller towns did not have a football team. You probably can't find a school in Texas that, at least, doesn't play six-man football.

At school, we had one experience that could have cost Dick his scholarship. One has to remember that McMurry was a church-sponsored school, and Abilene was dry at that time. Beer runs were to nearby Breckenridge or Lowake near San Angelo. These locales were maybe one and one-half or two hours from school. One Friday, Dick and I had made a beer run to Lowake; and we were going to double date that evening. When we got back to Abilene, we iced down the beer in a canvas duffle bag and put it in the trunk of my car. We still had several hours to kill before we had to pick up our dates, so we decided to drive to nearby Clyde, Texas. It had been struck the night before by a tornado. We wanted to take a look at the damage. The trip over was uneventful and we quickly saw all we wanted, and perhaps more, of the tremendous damage which had all but wiped out Clyde. We hurried back to Abilene so we would not be late in picking up our dates. Unfortunately, as we were nearing the downtown section of Abilene on a one-way street, we were hit head on by a car full of drunks driving the wrong way. I had looked down to change the radio station for a couple of seconds, and when I looked up, I saw the headlights of a 1936 Chevrolet coming right at me. The resulting collision sent Dick into my windshield with enough force to put a small hole in the safety glass. He had an egg-sized knot on his forehead, but otherwise was fortunately all right. The local police had apparently been summoned by some bystander who heard or saw the crash.

They went about gathering statements and the like, but to Dick and me, it seemed like that they were moving at a snail's pace. What worried us was the dripping of water on to the road surface under the trunk area of my car caused by the ice melting in the canvas duffle bag. We had noticed this immediately after we got out of the car, but apparently no one else had yet seen it. How would we explain two McMurry students with a load of iced-down beer. Paticularly, how would we explain to the school, if we were charged with illegal possession, bootlegging or whatever, that two of its students were in jail? Equally as bad, what was its star basketball player doing drinking beer during season? How would we explain this to our parents especially if we were kicked out of school or suspended? Woe was us, especially since the puddle of water was getting bigger. Even the sound of the dripping water sounded to us like Niagara Falls, taking into account our state of mind and guilty consciences.

Well, the wrecker finally hooked on to the front of my car and towed it away. Now the water was clearly visible to everyone. In fact, one police officer asked the other why water was on the road that far back from the radiators of the two cars in the collision. Fortunately, he replied that he didn't know and shrugged it off to advise the driver of the other car that he was going to charge him with DWI and that he had to go to the station with them. Off they drove to the police station. It seemed like a minor miracle. We called one of the girls that we were dating that evening and she came and got us. However, we were in no mood to go out, so she took us back to the campus. Then it hit us that the wrecker company might see the leaking water at their downtown storage garage and open the trunk to see what was going on. We had already worried ourselves half to death over all the various scenarios of getting caught in this shenanigan, so any loose end at this time was terrifying. Thus we decided to get one of the guys in the dorm to drive us to the storage garage first thing the next morning and try to retrieve the duffle bag so we could dispose of the evidence once and for all. We could then go back to studying and playing basketball and all those good things.

We got to the garage the next morning and told them we needed to retrieve some of our belongings from the car trunk before the repair facility took possession of the car. The desk guy on duty recognized Dick and turned out to be a big McMurry basketball fan. While Dick talked to him and kept him occupied, I got the bag out of the trunk and into the car of our friend. We left and disposed of the bag and its contents at the first garbage container we spotted behind a store on the way back to school. We both said a silent prayer as this sorry saga came officially to an end. To this good day, I still have little taste for beer, as it always reminds me of this encounter of the closest kind.

As soon as school ended that semester, I said some hard goodbyes and went home to work for the summer months. For it was the last semester at McMurry and time to move on in the fall to the big city of Austin to attend the University of Texas.

Chapter V

THE UNIVERSITY

One of the difficult tasks I had when it was time to leave McMurry to attend the University of Texas, in Austin, was to break the news to my cousin, John Deffebach, who lived in Abilene with his wife Laura and managed the Burton Lingo Lumber Company office there until his retirement. A few might remember the Burton Lingo Lumber chain of stores located throughout Texas and their bright orange and black buildings. My grandfather also worked for Burton Lingo, managing yards in Snyder, Dennison Ranger and Tuscola until his retirement. In addition, my grandfather's brother and John's father, Arthur Deffebach, was the secretary-treasurer of Burton Lingo at its company headquarters in Fort Worth. All these Burton Lingo jobs were probably a result of my great-grandfather's (John Adam, who was killed by the Indians) brother, Daniel, marrying into the Burton family in 1881. Be that as it may, the fact was that John and Laura had been my parents away from home, and I was always welcome to go to their home near the McMurry campus for fellowship and food. They had two daughters, Carol and Jeanne, who also made me feel at home and important on these visits. It was hard enough to pull away from these wonderful people, who had made me feel so much at home, but there was another factor that made it more difficult.

Since the orange portion of the University of Texas official colors (orange and white) was shared by Burton Lingo, one might think my cousin John would be at least half thrilled with my announcement that I would be attending Texas University the following year. He was not. The problem was that he was a dyed-in-the-wool Aggie from Texas A&M. Worse still, he played end on their football team under the great coach, Dana X. Bible, and was captain of the team his senior year. This made his blood run maroon and white. He couldn't even spell orange. After a few choice remarks about how miserable I would be as a *teasip*—a term of affection used by Aggies to describe students of their sister state university—he allowed as how he had never had a relative who was so misguided as to even consider Texas as an educational institution. After having his say about my intentions, he soon calmed down and reasoned that there had to be a first time for everything, and perhaps Texas was not as bad as it was when it was their bitter rival at Texas A&M in his day some fifteen years or so before. This was a welcome turn in the conversation. Fortunately, at the time, I had not tasted the cabernet of the spirit and intensity of this rivalry or the conversation could have gotten much worse. As a parting gift, he gave me Jeremiah Deffebach's family Bible. Since Jeremiah was my great-great-grandfather and his Bible contained many entries in the family history section, this was and still is a priceless possession.

When fall rolled around, I was off to Austin, along with my good friend from high school, Jack Gorman, who had also attended another college for two years before transferring to Texas. We shared a room together in an apartment and both pledged Kappa Alpha fraternity that year. With twenty-five thousand students, it helped to belong to some group, if for no other reason than to have something in common with others who knew their way around the gigantic forty-acre campus. Once school started, it was big-time football, football and more football. To this day, there is no sport more exciting to me than college football. Even college basketball excites me more than its professional version. This is probably due to fact that nearly anything in the unexpected category can and usually does happen in a closely contested college game.

I was enrolled in the University's School of Business Administration, which was then one of the best in the nation. It had professors like John Arch White and George Hillis Newlove, who wrote the textbooks for subjects like elementary, intermediate and advanced auditing and cost accounting that many, if not most, of the major colleges and universities around the country then used in their curriculum. My dad had once again laid out my course of study to complete in two years the requirements to receive a bachelor of business administration degree with a major in public accountancy. In those days, that was a tough schedule, and it was compounded by my fascination with Texas football. It was also complicated by fraternity activities and girls. Remember, I had been raised in a small town where dancing was sinful. I could not imagine the action that went on in this university town. It was very different than anything I was used to. But I felt it was my duty to learn something about this lifestyle of the teasips, of which my cousin John had spoken.

To make matters worse, Marvin and Joe Sentell from Snyder joined Jack Gorman and me at Texas during our senior year. The four of us decided to rent a house in west Austin and share the fun and expenses. It worked out well for our needs, but it created quite a cultural shock to the previously laid back and quiet neighborhood. It was a great place to live, but a hard place to study. In short, these two years of undergraduate school only produced a B average, which was my lowest academic performance to date. In looking back on it, I realize it could have been much worst. A lot of things came natural to me, but others were foreign. For example, in my senior year I took advanced cost accounting from George Hillis Newlove, a professor with an international reputation. It was not necessary for my degree or major; and about 80 percent of the class consisted of certified public accountants who worked in Austin and were only auditing the course. Professor Newlove, on the first day of class, opined that if they gave an examination for president of the United States, we would be looking at him. Then he turned to the blackboard that surrounded the four walls of the classroom and started writing about Standard, Method A, and Method B of cost accounting. This is the kind of stuff that major manufacturers and the like have to worry about, not the little retail businesses I knew in Snyder. It was usually a mystery hour since he was always talking to the blackboard, rather than directly facing the class. I dutifully kept the best notes I could from his scribbling on the board before he vigorously erased them. He apparently had some concern somebody from the outside world might view his thoughts for reasons unknown. Thus, my notes were not always complete. In addition, I swear he had never taken third-grade handwriting from anybody like Mrs. Hornsberry in Snyder who made you practice slashes and ovals endlessly. I guess the professor must have thought that if an exam were given for president, it would not be necessary for someone to be able to read his writing in order to grade it.

Unfortunately, our exam rolled around. I had been home for a weekend and I visted with my dad's partner, Russell Yorgesen about my concern for this upcoming exam in advanced cost accounting. As it turned out, he had taken the course from Professor Newlove while at Texas. He granted it would be tough and warned me that the majority of the class had flunked when he was there. I was worried enough and Russell's comment didn't make me feel any better about my odds in passing. I had never flunked a course in my life, not even Spanish at McMurry which had been taught by a visiting eighty-year-old professor, Professora Benge, of the University of Mexico City. She also mumbled, but in *Spanish*, from the start of the *beginners* class. If it had not been for a good textbook, I could have easily flunked that course as only two of us passed it anyway, myself (by maxing out the written part of the final due to practically memorizing the text book for the final) and Lila Winters, a classmate who had taken three years of Spanish in high school.

Advanced cost accounting, however, loomed as a greater challenge. Russell ended our discussion with an afterthought about an unforeseen question on Newlove's exam that almost wiped him out. One of the test problems to solve consisted of being given the *answer* to a Method A or B cost accounting problem, and the assignment was to determine what the *question* was that would produce the answer. Now that sounded like something a frustrated college professor who thought he ought to be the president of the United States would do. So when I went back to school from my weekend visit to Snyder, I practiced doing cost accounting methods backwards to guard against this revolting contingency.

I didn't have much else to do but to read my incomplete notes, which were beginning to look like I had taken them in Spanish or some other foreign language. Amazingly, God was with me as the exam only consisted of three problems; the last was weighted 50 percent of the exam and stated the *answer* to a Method B cost accounting problem and required we determine the *question* that would produce that answer. The audible moaning in the exam room brought a smile to the professor's face, as he anticipated he had once again baffled a room full of mostly practicing CPAs. There were four passing grades as I recall and most importantly to me, I was one of the survivors who probably understood less cost accounting than any of those failing. But once in a while, it does seem better to be lucky than skillful.

The only other really close call that I had at Texas was a business law course I took in the summer session of my junior year. To complete my major and to be prepared to sit for the law portion of the CPA exam, I needed to take this course and had not been able to schedule it earlier due to conflicts with accounting courses. Thus, I stayed over for the summer session after my Snyder roommates had left for a summer of

R&R in quiet Snyder. I moved into an apartment complex known as the *Peso House* with Johnny Allred of Wichita Falls, who was also a Kappa Alpha and had used up his football eligibility. Johnny had played end for Texas, and he stayed over as he also needed this course to graduate. His dad was a practicing CPA in his home town and Johnny's uncle had been a governor of Texas. He was a great guy, and since we were only taking one course that summer, we had a *ball* that lasted all summer and up to about 2AM of the morning of the business law final.

We had been on an outing on Lake Austin, and when we came back to our room at the Peso House that early morning, we decided it was time to study for the exam later the same morning. We hit the books and our notes so hard that we fell asleep on top of them. The exam was scheduled at 8 AM, and we slept right through it. Later, upon awakening, panic set in. We got dressed and made a beeline to the business school to see if we could find the professor teaching the course. Fortunately, he was still in his office and was very surprised to see our shining faces. It was hard to explain to him what had happened; so we beat around the bush and told him about getting in late that night because we had to help care for a sick friend. There was an element of truth in this, as one of the guys with us at the lake that night had become ill from excessive drinking of Orange Blossom Punch (orange juice and vodka); and we had cleaned him up some before leaving. We pleaded with the professor to schedule an early makeup exam. His response was that he had travel plans for the rest of the summer. Things did not look good, especially for me.

Of course, he knew of Johnny as a former member of the Texas football team, but he didn't know me from Adam. By stroke of luck, he did seem interested in my surname and then asked if I was possibly related to Lura Dickinson who had been the school beauty at Texas Christian University when he was in school there. He thought she had married a football player from Texas A&M with a name similar to mine. He admitted that he had always had a secret crush on her. I was quick to tell the professor that not only did I know Lura, but she was married to my cousin, John; and that I had spent gobs of time in their home while at McMurry. During the next fifteen minutes or so, our request for a makeup exam was put on hold until he asked me tons of questions about how Lura was doing and how much family she had and the like. Home run! He ended the discussion by saying not only that he understood and admired our need to care for an ill buddy, but also that he was willing to let us take the makeup exam right then so that we would not lose any time and thus our late-hour studying would not be wasted. When the grades were posted, both Johnny and I were amazed that we both made As. At that time, I decided that it was better to be skillful in the law than it was just to be plain lucky. After all, it had been predestined that my next stop was law school, due to my dad's fixation that the lawyers were trying to steal the tax practice from accountants.

I settled down some for my senior year at Texas. My grades improved and football season was not as good as the year before. But life went on. During my final semester at Texas, I was married in April to Joan Matthews, whom I had met that fall in a business statistics class. Her father was a colonel in the air force. Her mother and father had divorced at an early age, and Joan lived with each from time to time before enrolling in Texas. Her mother lived and worked in Houston.

These were the days when families expected their kids to marry after college and start a family so they could have grandchildren. Particularly this was this true in small towns like Snyder. Also before graduating from business school, I sat in Austin for three parts of the CPA exam: theory, auditing and business law. I passed these parts. Before qualifying for a CPA license, I would have to have a full year of experience under the direction of a certified public accountant and pass the practice section of the exam. So after marriage and graduation, we headed back to Snyder where I was going to work under the supervision of my dad's partner, Russell Yorgesen to hack away at the experience requirement. I knew that it was doubtful that I could complete the full year's requirement at that time, since I was either going to start law school in the fall or deal with my military draft situation. I had finished my last semester at Texas with a student deferment. But, at least I could get three or four months of credit on the CPA requirement and then complete it when the situation permitted.

Chapter VI

UNITED STATES MARINE CORPS

As mentioned before, my dad's educational plans for me included law school. However, when I returned home in the summer of 1952, having graduated from the University of Texas undergraduate business school, I found that the local draft board was hot and heavy for my body, as up to that time I had been granted a student deferment. The Korean conflict (June 25, 1950-July 27, 1953) was dragging on and in the summer of 1952 no end was in sight. Our draft board was not exactly *local*, since it was located in Sweetwater, not in Snyder. Rumors were hot and heavy that the Snyder boys and ones from other small communities in the area were being picked sooner than the residents of Sweetwater boys. Whether true or not, I cannot say, but that story was making all the rounds in our small town. Thus, it was decision time, as I saw it, my options were to enroll in law school for the fall and extend my student deferral (hopefully), do nothing and get drafted into the walking army or apply to the U.S. Navy Officer's Candidate School and cruise and tool around the Pacific or wherever. The latter appealed to me, since I did not feel I could do justice to law school until I matured sufficiently to give law school my best academic shot. In any event, I did not want to give the Sweetwater draft board the satisfaction of shipping me off to the army. I had already been given a preinduction physical and exam in San Antonio soon after the draft for Korea had started and before I had been granted a student deferment. Everybody that showed up passed both the physical and written intelligence exam. That indicated to me that they were desperate for bodies since several of the guys sitting around me had indicated that they could not read.

The die was cast. I immediately got off my request letter to attend the next session of the Navy's Officer Candidate School at Newport Beach. That sounded like a nice relaxing place to study to become a naval officer and to cruise all over the world. The reply that I received was not directly from the navy, but rather from General Lemuel Shepherd, the then commandant of the Marine Corps. Since we had not previously been pen pals, I was very anxious to see how he had heard of me. The letter said, in so many words, that my OCS application for the navy had been passed on to him, since the navy had no immediate openings that would save me from the draft. He also said something about the exclusivity of his club, and they only needed a *few good men*. I thought it over as time was short, and I decided to accept membership in his exclusive organization as I had heard that it was a kissing cousin of the navy and was even older in point of seniority. The bottom line was that this decision would send a message to the Sweetwater draft board, and after all this invitation had been personally signed by the commandant of the Marine Corps. It probably would not be long before I would actually get to meet him, since his letter was so personal and he seemed so interested in my future.

It did not take long to receive my orders to report to Quantico, Virginia in the early part of September 1952. I got to Fredericksburg, Virginia a day early and checked into a motel. It was a Sunday night and I saw my first television ever—the *Ed Sullivan Show*. I was impressed although there was a fair amount of snow on the TV screen. Still it was a first, and surely a good sign for the success of the new career I was about to embark on the next morning in Quantico. I reported as ordered and could not wait to see the facilities for an officer candidate. Strangely, they looked just like those down the street for the enlisted men. Anyway, no time was wasted in giving all those reporting for duty shots, a haircut that was more like a shave and interesting clothing to wear, including shoes, socks, underwear, fatigues and a couple of khaki uniforms. From there we were shown our bunks and lockers. We stowed our equipment and gear, and then were told to relax until our drill instructor came that evening for *introductions*. This looked like it might even be better than the navy—at least at this point in time. Everybody was so polite and helpful. There were hundreds of people reporting with us, and everyone started to introduce themselves to those assigned to nearby bunks. It became apparent that the bunk and building assignments had been made alphabetically. I was surrounded by a number of the previous year's Notre Dame's football team. Amazingly, they had four or five players with surnames starting with *D*, like Dominich, Doble, etc. Nice guys but big and tough looking. Since we had not found any TV sets, a few poker games began; and we were enjoying this low-key indoctrination to the Marine Corps.

Then all hell broke out, and we met the devil in the form of our assigned drill instructor (DI), Sergeant Pellizaria. He stood us at attention. Most of us were in our underwear when he showed up. He told us we looked like a pile of horse manure, and that it was doubtful if any of us would finish the course. We were too soft, dumb and appeared to have too much education to lead real men. Later, we found out that he had just returned from Korea via the Naval Hospital on base where he had recovered from taking several .50-caliber sized-slugs in the belly from a Korean machine gun. It certainly must have been this experience that caused him to toss all his people and social skills to the wind. Nobody, I mean nobody, could hate people they had just met as much as he seemed to hate us. He told us to hit the showers and then the sack; and to report in uniform the next morning at 4:30 AM on the Potomac River side of the barracks. Private Dominich made a fatal mistake of asking him if chow was before or after this formation. His answer would never pass any censor, but I think he said the bottom line was neither. And if looks could count, Private Dominich would have been dead at that point.

The next morning, we fell out and found Sergeant Pellizaria waiting. He had us form several lines and then gave brief instructions on various commands, like "fall in, attention, about-face, at ease, parade rest" and the like. One poor soul was ten minutes late, and he was sent to report to the office of the company commander, Colonel Raymond Murray, who also had just returned from duty in Korea. It was said that he had been involved in the marines' strategic withdrawal from Inchon, a low point in Marine Corps history. The late offender never returned to the barracks; and we were later told that this meant, as we would too often see in the next ten weeks, that he was put on the next available train to the boot camp at Camp Pendleton in California. As one who went there as a result of dismissal from OCS, he would be given top priority for an early boat ticket to Korea. Private Doble nearly met the same fate that morning, in that Sergeant Pellizaria noticed his pajama bottoms sticking out beneath his fatigues. From the dressing down he got from our DI, I gathered that such behavior is not only frowned upon, but also must come close to being a capital offense. At least, Private Doble did not have to go directly to Korea via Camp Pendleton as a private. But it was soon apparent to all of us in the next several weeks that the DI had his gun sights on Doble, as he could seldom do anything right in his eyes. We were then given a series of exercises to perform while still in formation. After that, Sergeant Pellizaria headed us out on the road for a morning run. Finally, after we had been with him several hours that morning, he marched us in lock step to the chow hall. I am sure most of us had given up that food was even an option with him.

After breakfast, he introduced us to the obstacle course. It was a wonder to behold. It filled a space about the equivalent of a football field, and every form of torture device known to man was incorporated in it. The first obstacle looked easy. There were a number of metal poles laid across a twenty-yard-long expanse of water. The poles were mounted horizontally on top of vertical supports that caused the horizontal poles to be about eight or nine feet above the level of the water to be crossed. The idea was to run at a pole, jump up and wrap both hands around it and then walk with your hands, one over the other and so on, until you reached the other side. It wasn't too hard to do it if your initial jump resulted in a good hold of the crossing pipe with both hands. Some did not have the upper arm strength to make any forward progress, but the vast majority of our guys did. The devil is in the details. What we could not see, but soon encountered crossing the waterway, was the fact that the last six or eight feet of the crossing pipe was greased. Then, you had to have extremely fast hands to make any forward progress at all without losing your grip and falling into the water. The rest of the course had numerous high barricade hurdles, some with rope to pull yourself up and over with, but with some you had to get over them without any rope assist. There was barbed wire to crawl under; and on occasion, there was real bullets being shot just over the crawl area. But the worst part of running the obstacle course was that far too often, the drill instructor decided at the end of the course to start all over again. Not the first day, but there were many days thereafter that following a forced march of ten, fifteen or twenty miles, we would stop at the obstacle course for a turn or two on the way to our barracks. Sergeant Pellizaria may not have been the meanest man on earth, but he'd be somewhere in the top ten. At least, that was our opinion at the time.

Another neat event to test our resolve was a rope climb up a seven-story building. This was not only a test of physical conditioning but also was a quick vertigo check. Halfway up the first time we made this climb, I decided that the last thing

I would do, no matter what, was to look down at where I had been. Instead, I concentrated on where I had to go. In addition, people were yelling at you from both the top and bottom of the building, particularly the drill instructor. When I made it to the top the first time, I found out something else we had not been told. The rope was not anchored physically to the roof of the building. Instead, you were in the hands of two marines sitting on the top of the building who anchored the rope. Each two of the OCS candidates that ascended replaced the two others who had anchored their climb. This was somewhat akin to packing parachutes for a drop from a practice tower, but never knowing who actually packed the one you were wearing. Later, we found this was an important and realistic lesson in teamwork. On a climb, I had reached the roof, saw the two marines on top and pulled myself over the ledge of the roof. When I turned to look at the guys anchoring the rope, I saw Private Abercombie just as he reached the ledge of the roof and then made the mistake of looking down at the ground. His eyes rolled up and he either passed out or simply couldn't hold on; but the result was a seven-floor fall and he landed on his back. Looking down at him lying motionless on the ground, I knew he must be dead. They hauled him off in an ambulance, and nobody would tell us anything. This was not totally uncommon as we had office candidates expire just from running, doing the obstacle course or a combination of both activities. We never heard any details or mention of them again. However in this case, we were told by a senior officer after we completed OCS that he had survived and was repeating the course with the next group that was to follow us. It was amazing that he survived that fall.

Another of our drill instructor's fun and game activities was a weekly ballot among our platoon to determine who the week's biggest *screwups* were. Regardless, of other disqualifying events for weekend liberty (which wasn't even available until our fifth week in OCS), such as rifle check on

Saturday morning's formation, bed check each morning (sheets and blanket so taunt that the DI could bounce a quarter on them), shoe shines and general condition of each person's area, the top three vote getters for *screwup* of the week were not entitled to liberty. Important as this was, you can imagine how intense the politics became. Naturally, everyone tried to vote for whomever had been chewed out the most by the DI during the week. Since those who qualified in that category were already in trouble with the DI, the weekend vote would normally make him happy by confirming his reason for chewing these guys out in the first place; and it probably didn't actually affect these guys liberty status anyway. The DI would have probably nailed them anyway that week by finding their rifle dirty or their living quarters unsatisfactory.

So went life in weeding out the unqualified for the commandant's apparent search for just a *few good men*. Fortunately, I got along with my fellow candidates and usually was able to keep from incurring Sergeant Pellizaria's wrath; therefore, once liberty was available, I enjoyed weekend leave, and normally we spent it in Washington, DC. There were hundreds of things for a country boy to enjoy in our nation's capitol. Besides all the monuments and museums, we even saw a stage show featuring Patti Page.

About the fifth week into OCS and about the time everyone began to wonder if they were going to be able to make it through the course, I received an official envelope in the daily mail call that had been forwarded to me from home. It was from the Department of Navy and advised me that I had been accepted in Naval Officers Candidate School, commencing the next week. I was elated as I had now had some doubt of my original reasoning that the USMC was just a kissing cousin of the navy. I was sure that the navy's version of OCS would be a breeze compared to what we had been going through at Quantico. When I next glimpsed Sergeant Pellizaria nearby, I approached him with my orders and told him what I had in hand. I also told him I was very disappointed to leave his quality training program, but orders were orders. He took the orders and after a quick look at them, he tore them up, threw them away and declared that he was happy I was disappointed to leave because I was going to stay. I asked him what I should do about a response to the orders, and he informed me that he had disposed of them and not to worry. I had no choice, so I didn't worry; and nobody from the navy ever came to put me in the brig or anything like that. So I guess he was right or he reported it later to someone who contacted the navy. I will never know.

However, I will never forget our observance of Thanksgiving that year. We had a special formation and marched to the mess hall not knowing what to expect. When we got there we were dismissed outside the mess hall to go inside. Table after table was laid out with a huge amount of turkey and all the trimmings. We all looked at each other like we had died and gone to heaven. This bore no resemblance to the stuff ordinarily we had to stand in long lines for and have dipped on our plates. We were able to take seats at any table with the food just sitting there and waiting for us. There was one slight quirk. There were no napkins or tableware at any table. We, therefore, had to eat with our hands and had nothing to wipe them with but our fatigues. Pretty gross, but the worst was yet to come. When an appropriate amount of time had elapsed to eat, we were ordered to form outside; and then we were marched to the movie facility. For the next two hours, we were shown actual combat footage from island landings in the Pacific during World War II. It was bloody and gory, full of marines being blown apart in all kinds of ways. With a full belly, it left a lasting impression on all of us to see the most graphic blood and gut footage we had ever seen. If the special food had momentarily blinded us to where we were and what we were learning to do here, we were certainly brought back to reality in a hurry.

We then had another daily activity added to supplement the obstacle course. The DI would set a barrel on the ground and we would line up and jump headfirst over it and the idea was to land on your shoulder and roll forward to land hopefully on your feet. After everyone in his group had cleared one barrel, he put another one behind it, which doubled the area you would have to clear. A third barrel would be added, which was about the max that anyone could clear by going headfirst over the barrel(s). Of course, not everyone had the same ability to clear the barrels by jumping headfirst over them, so there were often collisions with them. There were also some injuries that sent the injured to sick bay. My observation was that a trip to the sick bay was usually a one-way ticket out of our class. Reportedly, those guys were given one more chance in the next OCS class; and failing to graduate then, for whatever reason (sick or injured etc.), they were shipped out to Pendleton, then to Korea.

Unfortunately, I had a bad collision with the third barrel during the last week of OCS. I sustained a separated shoulder or what felt like one. I knew better than to report to sick bay this late in the game, because about the last thing I wanted at that point was to start over in the next class. So I decided to fake it for this last week. That was nearly my undoing, because any pressure such as shouldering a rifle or any activity on the obstacle course that required both arms shot enough pain through the shoulder to bring me to the brink of passing out. I actually was able to make it over the water on the pole, using the fastest one hand grasp I could muster to get across or at least far enough across so as not to have to repeat it. Fortunately, the DI had become lax over the last week or so in greasing that pole, which made it easier to cross; and otherwise I do not believe that I could have done it with the use of only one hand and arm.

The real test came the last day of class. The agenda was a twenty-five-mile march with full pack and armament. Unfortunately, I was assigned a Browning Automatic Rifle (BAR) for a weapon rather than a M1 rifle or a carbine. The BAR weighed much more and unfortunately it was my right shoulder that was injured. We were supposed to carry our weapon slung over the right shoulder. Woe was me! But the good news, if any and however slight, it was a night march and the moon was only at quarter level. During the march, I was occasionally able to switch the BAR to my left shoulder without the DI noticing it. My buddies did, however, and began putting two and two together as to why I had gotten so quiet and looked so pale the last several days. The first thing I knew one after the other in our squad would take the BAR and carry it for a few miles while I carried their piece, a rifle or carbine. Particularly, the latter felt like a toothpick after shouldering the BAR for a time. Bear in mind that everyone had a full pack on their back also. It was amazing to me how much of a team we had become over the ten weeks and how much respect for each other had developed, notwithstanding the negative voting technique employed for weekly liberty. I truly do not believe that I would have made the full twenty-five mile hike if they had not come to my aid. Also, I do not believe that the DI didn't see what was going on. Maybe he had decided to look the other way, since he knew I had hurt the shoulder when it happened and perhaps gave me some credit for not heading for sick bay. Regardless, I will never know. But the next day, I made the graduating list, also notifying us that the listed personnel would be commissioned second lieutenants in the USMC the next day.

All the news was not so happy, as a number of our class members were not listed. We never saw those who exited at that point. Their names had been called out at roll call, and they were marched directly to Colonel Murray's office for whatever purpose. Rumor had it that he gave each man a chance to briefly state his case, which he considered and apparently usually rejected. In any event, they were not present nor were they commissioned the following day. It was now a week or so before Christmas, and after lying around our bunks for a day and playing poker, we were given leave for the holidays. We were to report back in January, as a second lieutenant, to the USMC basic infantry school in Quantico. We were also told to stop in Washington, DC, on the way out or on the way back and purchase our basic officer's uniforms.

While home during the break from OCS to basic infantry school, I weighed for the first time since I initially reported for duty. I had then weighed 205 pounds and was in reasonably good shape. After ten weeks in OCS, I weighted 168 pounds. This was going to have to be the benchmark for the rest of my career in the marines, because before I returned to Quantico, I had spent an afternoon in Washington buying the minimum requirement of my officer's uniforms. I had to hold my weight to that level in order not to have to return for alterations or to purchase larger sizes of the same items. I was now a tall drink of water like my junior high teacher, Ms. Jones, who had warmed by backside for me taking target practice at hers with a spit ball.

Basic infantry school was a six-month course and would involve day and many night exercises as well as classroom work at Quantico. However, you could live anywhere in the vicinity that was practical to get to and from work. You no longer would be imprisoned 24-7 by the USMC. I chose, as did several of my friends, to live in Fredericksburg, Virginia, which was about twenty-five miles south of Quantico. The drive took about forty-five minutes each way. Fredericksburg was fairly small at that time and was very peaceful. Three of us lived in the same apartment complex, and therefore, we could car pool. One of the first purchases I made upon returning to this area was a 13 inch Motorola TV; as I still had only seen television one time and that was in Fredericksburg the night before I originally reported to Quantico for OCS.

During basic infantry school, my daughter, Susan, was born at the U.S. Naval Hospital at Quantico. My parents came up from Snyder, and my dad was so concerned that his first grandchild was not going to be a native Texan; he brought a box filled with Texas soil with him. After rather extensive negotiating with the naval duty officer of the day in the birthing area, my dad persuaded him to permit the box of Texas soil to be placed underneath the birthing table, thereby creating the contention that she was born on or at least over Texas soil. The navy's total charge to me for the prenatal and delivery services was $25 and the Texas soil was returned to my dad to boot.

The six months in infantry school seemed to go very fast, whereas the ten weeks before in OCS seemed like a lifetime. This pointed up the fact that once commissioned, training was more civilized and emphasis was on weapons, leadership, chain of command, engagement strategy, military organization and numerous field exercises to practice tactics we learned in the classroom. About the worst duty during this period of time would be night field problems. We nearly always had to dig foxholes in which to sleep, what little we had; and this was often complicated by disturbing a den of hibernating Virginia timber rattlesnakes. What this usually meant was a strategic relocation of the foxhole and starting to dig all over again. This further diminished the time available for a few winks before the next phase of the exercise commenced.

As our basic infantry training approached its completion, classroom activity increased with a lot of emphasis on *Semper Fi*, *esprit di corps*, and general review of the *few and the proud* history of the corps. A number of us were also sent to Washington to observe and act as an honor guard in a special parade which ended with a concert of the United States Marine Band. Morale was high as the band concluded with John Philip Sousa's "Stars & Stripes Forever." Sousa is reported as once saying, "March music is for the feet, not for the head." But this song has become more of a rallying source of our nation mentally marching together toward a common goal. It is especially lifting when it is played by a great band; and the marine band is among the greatest.

Soon we were meeting almost daily as it was time to request assignments for active duty posts. It seemed that all the weeks in OCS and months in basic infantry training were beginning to come together. We had watched each other grow up mentally, physically and develop into a cohesive group of men, and indeed we were mentally marching toward a common goal. When the requests for duty were tallied, our company to the man had put *Korea* as our first preference for duty. Talk about brainwashing through propaganda, turkey dinners, blood and gut films and other tactics; it had all contributed to this state of mind that to an outsider would have been considered akin to insanity. Harry Truman once alluded to the Marine Corps as having a propaganda machine second to none. A retired general officer has been quoted somewhat more graphically as describing (tongue in cheek I am sure) a Marine fire team as containing *one shooter, one looter and two photographers* (reported by Cpl. John J. Papietro, USMC Retired, at *www.grunt.com).*

In any event, over our brief tenure with the *few and the proud* our company had been successfully indoctrinated to understand that a military operation requires absolute and unquestioned discipline and teamwork. We had learned this lesson over time, and I must say that in retrospect I understand Sergeant Pellizaria and all the other hardships we had encountered had a purpose. In combat, there is no time to learn how to then obey orders; it must be so ingrained in you that it is automatic.

We next received our first duty station orders. Few actually went to Korea directly. I was ordered to report in late June 1953 to the commanding officer, 1stAAW Battalion, Camp Lejeune, North Carolina. AA stood for antiaircraft, but I didn't have a clue at that time that the marines had such an organization, although I realized that all marines are trained first and foremost for infantry duty regardless of final specialization in some related field.

Chapter VII

ACTIVE DUTY ASSIGNMENTS

Several of us reported to Camp Lejeune at the same time, including my good friend, Pete Booth. He and his wife were one of the several couples who shared the same apartment complex in Fredericksburg while we attended basic infantry school at Quantico. Base housing at Camp Lejeune for married junior grade officers was nonexistent, and they had to scrape the barrel for inexpensive housing in nearby Jacksonville, North Carolina.

If you do not have resources, it sometimes helps to have friends who do. Pete was married to a girl from Rocky Mount, North Carolina whose father was a prominent doctor. Among other things, the family had a beach house at Topsail Beach, just a short drive from the marine base. Pete's in-laws were so kind as to offer him and his wife, Sybil, the use of the beach house while awaiting base housing. The beach house had two stories, and they decided that it would be a good ideal if we occupied one floor and they the other. What a great deal! It was so hot and humid at Camp Lejeune during the summer months that we had to change uniforms at noon. To then be able to come home from work at the base to the comforts of a first-class beach house on a first-class beach made us the envy of all our fellow junior officers, as well as a few field grade officers who didn't have it this good with base housing. It was a ritual that Pete and I would come home in the early evening, change to our swimming trunks and then hit the water for a cooling-down period. Then we would relax on the beach with a beer or two and discuss the day's work problems, if any, before dinner that night.

We were both assigned as platoon leaders to an antiaircraft battalion that was in the state of transition. Its mission was to convert the use of its primary weapons to provide direct ground support for the front lines in Korea. We were equipped with hand-me-down army World War II halftracks with quad .50-caliber machine guns and Walker Bulldog light tanks with twin .40mm cannons. The idea was that they were to be used to lay down ground fire in front of our battle lines that would make it difficult for the gooks to penetrate our lines, particularly at night. Besides all the .50-caliber rapid fire from the machine guns, the .40mm cannons from the tanks would be like lobbing hand grenades at the approximate rate of 240 a minute. The downside of the concept was the weight of our battalion. Not only do you have the mechanized vehicles to deal with, but also a mass of spare parts to keep the old World War II equipment repaired and functioning. The order of the day was to get the weight down to a minimum, train the personnel to be proficient at firing at the ground targets instead of aircraft and get to Korea as soon as possible. However, the battalion was in limbo at this time, since it was awaiting the completion of a remodel of an old air force base in Twentynine Palms, California. Then when complete, they were going to transfer the battalion in mass to the new location, as it would have sufficient space to accommodate extensive weapons training and the development of ground support firing techniques. It would also be nearer to the staging area on the West Coast for embarkation to Korea. However, during this hiatus, the Korean cease-fire agreement was signed on July 27, 1953. This officially ended hostilities; however, it was a nervous truce and renewed emphasis was placed on making the California move as soon as possible.

At Camp Lejeune, one of my first extra assignments was to serve as one of the three members of the battalion's special court martial board. I thought at first that they must have found out that I had taken business law in college. However, it was clear at the first court martial called by the presiding officer of the board that experience in business law, or criminal law for that matter, wasn't a job requirement. It went like this. I walked into the hearing room and met the other two officers so assigned. One was a major, who was the battalion executive officer; and the other was a first lieutenant who commanded a line company. They very simply explained the rules to me, as I was a green second lieutenant getting ready to judge my first case. The major first reminded the assembled group that all cases we decided were automatically reviewed by the battalion commander, who was a bird colonel, and that his wisdom was obviously superior to ours. He stated that if the facts of the case indicated a defendant needed any slack cut in verdict or sentencing, it would be the prerogative of the commanding officer to do so. Then to summarize what he had just propounded, the major said, "Bring in the next guilty bastard so we can hang him. Do you understand?" And that was the way it worked. Fortunately, we didn't have too many severe matters brought before this fair and impartial tribunal while I served.

I was just settling into the routine at enjoying Topsail Beach and hoping nobody did anything bad enough to be brought before the special court martial board, when I was ordered in August 1953 to report to the commanding officer of the battalion. He advised me that I and another second lieutenant from his command were being specially assigned, preceding the battalion's transfer to California, to the army's antiaircraft and guided missile school for field grade officers at Fort Bliss, Texas. He said that his superior was looking down the road and wanted a couple of junior officer guinea pigs to enroll in the field grade officers' version of the training school at Fort Bliss. It seems it was only a ten-week school and the regular version of the school for junior grade officers required many months. Two things were therefore driving this assignment: assuming we could successfully compete with field grade officers and pass the short course, then (1) the USMC could save a lot of money and (2) it could substantially reduce officer training time in the specialized antiaircraft and guided missile facility. We were not overly concerned with guided missiles in our mission, but it was inseparable at the army base from the antiaircraft weaponry training. Since we really were not interested in shooting at airplanes with antiaircraft traditional weapons or guided missiles, I could only assume that somewhere in the ivory tower of the Marine Corps someone had declared some type of this training to be mandatory. Ours was not to question why, but only to do or die. We were dismissed with good wishes and a clear implication that flunking this school would not be a healthy career option.

I picked up the phone that evening and called home, to let the folks know we were coming back to Texas, at least temporarily. I also asked my dad if he had any contacts in El Paso since we were informed that base housing would not be available due to the short duration of the assignment. He said he would check out a few sources and let me know. He did in a day or two, advising that a friend of his had a brother in the real estate business in El Paso. He had been told that housing was in short supply everywhere in that city. There were very few apartment buildings at all and they were old. He had promised my dad to get back in touch with him as soon as his brother could survey availability. It was about time that we had to leave in order to timely report to the only other marine at Fort Bliss, a bird colonel serving as a liaison officer with the army with respect to marine personnel assigned in and out of the schools at that base. At the last minute, my dad called and said he had good news. As far as the real estate guy could tell, he had landed us the last available apartment in El Paso. The bad news is that it was in the central part of the city and not too convenient to the base. I told him to tell his friend that I would take it. My fellow officer who was being then assigned did not have any housing located, but he finally did manage to find housing in a motel that had been converted to monthly rentals because its physical appearance scared all the passing motorists looking for lodging and diverted them to other motels in the area.

When in El Paso, I was rather surprised that the apartment was better and more substantial than I had imagined. I supposed that the realtor brother of my father's contact must have had some stroke of luck to find it. It was several days before I noticed what appeared to be a bullet hole in the drywall behind the bed. I looked further and found what appeared to be dried blood on the floor near the hole in the drywall. I inquired of the apartment manager as to what it was that I had found. He seemed surprised that I had not been told that the only reason the apartment was available was due to the fact that a murder in it a short time ago created the vacancy. It turned out to be one that I had actually read about in a Jacksonville newspaper before we left there. A daughter of a wealthy Oklahoma family had married a guy in the service, who had been sent to El Paso. They had some type of big fight and the wife had shot her husband as he slept in the bed of that apartment. Because of the prominence of the girl's family, the story had received a lot of press with the implication that she had received some sort of special treatment from the local authorities when arrested. In any event, the story did not make the stay in El Paso very pleasant, not to mention the fact that the apartment turned out to be *air cooled* by fan. The only air conditioners in El Paso in the early 1950s were swamp coolers and they were not always available on the older buildings. You could install a *Mickey Mouse* window unit of that type, but that took a tenant's investment that I couldn't afford and still pay the rent.

The training class was really first class and my marine counterpart and I found that not only could we compete with the field grade army officers, but it was actually easy due to the fact that we had only been out of college a few years and many of the army officers were a lot older and rustier in the classroom. In any event we had a lot of fun firing weapons on the vast West Texas and New Mexico ranges available to the base, even though our targets were drones instead of ground targets. The marine liaison colonel told us that our CO back at our battalion was proud of the job we did, and that we were to receive some type of commendation for breaking ground in this assignment. As I recall, eventually a letter from him reached us, but no ribbons or anything tangible were attached. The liaison colonel, in early October 1953, also presented us with orders to report directly to the *about to open* marine base at Twentynine Palms, even though the battalion would not be there until about thirty days later. These orders amounted to thirty days' leave without assigned duties and with pay.

The other marine who came with me to Fort Bliss was going to spend the time at his home. I decided that it would be better to go on to the Twentynine Palms base and scout out housing and the lay of the land in general. This proved to be a good move. When I got to California and finally found the road from the freeway to Twentynine Palms, I noted that it was not going to be adjacent or too close to Palm Springs, the desert retreat for Hollywood stars and the like, because from the freeway you went south to Palm Springs but north over a mountain range to Twentynine Palms. These were not exactly *sister cities*. Once I arrived in Twentynine Palms, I went to the marine base which was not yet officially open, but did have a skeleton staff on duty. I was informed that while the working buildings and enlisted men's barracks had been completed and were ready for use; base housing for officers and married personnel was only partially complete but would be expanded significantly over the next several months. They also indicated that it would be assigned once the battalion move was made, as available and probably in order of seniority. Flash, another housing shortage was obvious! I then went into the small town itself to see what housing was available there, particularly since I needed something immediately. The answer was *not much* except a rundown small apartment complex and a few houses for rent. The rental listings at the local real estate officer were few and not very attractive. I drove through the residential areas, one by one, to see if anything might be under construction contemplating the opening of the base and not yet listed. Near the end of the day, lighting struck as I drove up to a duplex that was either recently completed or near completion.

There was no sign or any indication of the builder's name or that of the property's owner. I went next door to inquire. I met an extremely nice, elderly gentleman with a thick accent. He had immigrated to America some years before from the Netherlands and somehow ended up in this out-of-the-way place. He was a carpenter by trade and had personally built the duplex next door in anticipation of the opening of the new base. He had not listed it, as he was still adding up his building costs in order to determine what the monthly rentals of the two units would have to be. I told him I was extremely interested in not only one but both of the units, and I needed one immediately and the other within the next thirty days. This need worked out to be a perfect match for him, since one unit was complete and the other was about 95 percent complete, needing a small amount of woodwork and interior painting. Not only were these units new, but they had an amazing amount of cabinets and built-ins for the size of the units. This was due to his carpentry expertise. I knew that my best chance not to let these gems slip away was to make a deal on the spot and to take both units in order to sweeten the deal for him. Then, he would not have to list with a realtor or put up signs to handle renting them himself. I felt that he was a better craftsman than a businessman. Of course, there was a slight gamble involved on my part, because I knew I needed to lay off one unit within the next thirty days; failing to do so, I could not have afforded the rent on both.

Actually, he came up with a very reasonable rent on each unit and apologized for the fact it was higher than he had originally contemplated when launching the project. He had underestimated his costs, probably due to the extensive millwork and cabinetry not usually found in this type of rental unit. Compared to what I had found at the real estate office, the duplex at his price was a steal. We shook hands on the deal, and I made two phone calls as soon as I could. One was to Boomtown Furniture Company in Jacksonville, North Carolina, which was holding a *houseful* of furniture we had purchased upon arriving at Camp Lejeune and anticipating that we would have to rent an unfurnished house in Jacksonville. When the Topsail beach house was offered, it was furnished to the hilt and we made a deal with Boomtown to hold the furniture we had bought until we needed it. After all, we had spent a whopping $300 to buy furniture for a living room, kitchen and bedroom. They sounded happy to get rid of it as it had been taking up space for several months, and they agreed to ship it immediately. The other call was to Captain Jack Norman, who was the company commander of the unit in which I was a platoon leader at Camp Lejeune. He indicated that he had been trying to catch up with me at Fort Bliss, but had been unsuccessful as we had already left El Paso. I explained the housing situation at Twentynine Palms and what I had done. I told him he had first shot at the second duplex unit. He had been around the Marine Corps for some time, so he knew how screwed up the move was going to be with base housing being incomplete. He jumped on the opportunity and said that he would pick up the first month's rent even if he was not yet in Twentynine Palms at the time it came due. One must understand that it is hard to eliminate politics in any organization. I knew Jack had recommended me for an early promotion. He had a lot of influence with the battalion commander. Jack had been an enlisted marine in the later stages of the Pacific campaign in World War II and was combat tested.

It wasn't but several weeks until our battalion personnel commenced arriving in Twentynine Palms. The enlisted personnel came mainly in a group, but the officers came at different times and I cannot count the number of people who would stop by the duplex and inquire as to its availability. Many of them I knew, and they could not figure out how I had tied up the best housing in the area. One of the inquirers was the other marine who went with me to the Fort Bliss training school and decided to go home after completing the course. Now, he was a sick puppy for not coming with me directly to California. At least, he understood why Captain Norman had been give first crack at the second unit and was comforted by my telling him he would have been next on the list if Jack had declined the offer. I would have thought of him next, but I doubt that I could have made good on the offer as I did not know how to contact him at his home; and if someone came along first to take me off the hook on my commitment to the landlord for the rent on the second unit, I do not think I could have afforded to say no.

With the Korean conflict in the early stages of truce, our entire battalion's move to the desert of California was completed. Our training schedule was at first intense; however, as time passed it relaxed somewhat. Our battalion executive officer, Major Hemingway, probably had something to do with that, since his favorite saying was "You don't have to practice to be miserable." Major Hemingway was an old-timer who had held every rank in the USMC from private to major over about a twenty-year career and had seen lots of action during World War II. On the other hand, our commanding officer of the battalion had no combat experience and was a bird colonel from the Marine Corps reserves somewhere around Boston. I never did verify it, but I was told by several of the officers who had been fairly close to him that he sold shoes and shoe strings in civilian life. In any event, he loved night problems in the Mojave Desert and forced marches into the mountains around the base in order to control his excessive weight. Of course, he carried only a .45-caliber pistol and no pack. Everyone else was fairly loaded down with weapons and equipment. During this time of fun and games, I was promoted to first lieutenant and became a company commander. This was more responsibility but also meant more pay.

I think one reason that the major was able to reduce *practicing to be miserable* had to do with an incident that occurred on the parade grounds when our battalion had fallen out in full strength to greet General Hart, our supreme commander who was then stationed in Hawaii. He was making his first inspection tour of the newly opened base. Our CO, being a conservative shoe salesman from Boston, didn't want to take any chances with not being ready for General Hart's arrival. His ETA was only an estimate due to the fact he was flying in from Hawaii that day. Accordingly, the Colonel had us in formation at about 8 AM, standing on a field of asphalt adjoining the landing strip. We were in summer khaki uniforms, tie and all. Most of the time, he had everyone at parade rest, not at ease. I guess he thought the general might suddenly appear in the sky and he wouldn't be able to bring the troops to full attention in time to keep the general from observing the activity while landing. I do not have a clue as to the actual reason, since none of the events of that morning made any sense. It was extremely hot and we stood in formation without shade or water on the hot asphalt from 8 AM until the General finally appeared at about 11:30 AM. This took its toll, as some of the troops actually passed out and had to be carried off during the morning. Others had huge bands of sweat showing on their khaki shirts. But the biggest casualty of all turned out to be the colonel, who wet his pants about the time the general was disembarking from his aircraft. And, of course, the colonel was out in front as the first person in the formation to greet the general. So here was our leader in all his glory and pee stains visible from his crotch to the bottom of his pants. Not only could this be seen from his front, but also from his backside by the troops. You had to listen carefully, but a good deal of tittering could be heard throughout the formation.

I was not privy to what passed between the general and the colonel, but the general cut short the ceremony and did not conduct a full inspection of all the troops assembled. Instead, he and the colonel got in a jeep and made a beeline to the colonel's office. I was told that they had a long discussion there and the general then made an abbreviated inspection of the physical plant and flew out ahead of his scheduled departure. The colonel was seldom seen after that, even at the officers' club where he usually hung out. The major's influence then seemed much greater, and that's why I think the intensity of our training relaxed, particularly night problems, which required sleeping with the sidewinder rattle snakes of the Mojave Desert, and forced marches in and over the mountains during the day. We spent much more time learning to fire our quad .50s and twin .40s accurately at ground targets during the day and sometimes at night, but we seldom had to sleep with the snakes after that eventful formation for General Hart.

In addition to a better life on the base, during work hours and off, it became increasing clear during 1954 that the Korean truce was fairly secure for the time being and that our mission would only effect future conflicts of one type or the other. My active duty commitment was close to expiring, although I had no doubt that it could be extended if anything heated up anywhere in the world. In any event, someone determined that they could get along without those of us who had not chosen the Marine Corps as a career, and I was separated from active duty effective December 1, 1954. I was still committed to a total of eight years in the USMCR, less my active duty time.

However, thereafter, they changed the rules to permit anyone who had met their active duty requirement to either retire, if eligible, or be honorably discharged at rank with no further inactive reserve requirement unless they wanted to actively participate in a reserve unit somewhere in their area. I could not do the latter since I would not be accepted by the commanding officer of the reserve unit in Austin, Texas where I was to attend law school. I had already checked that possibility because I wanted the extra money during school. The problem was that I had been promoted to captain before the commanding officer in Austin; and, therefore I would be senior in rank and he didn't want to lose his command. Since I was not eligible for retirement, I was honorably discharged as a captain in the USMCR. If this quirk in the rules and regulations had not occurred, I am sure that I would have remained in the reserves and been called back into active duty during some phase of the Vietnam operation. As my law practice would have probably been affected, my career plan and perhaps my life might have been altered. Somebody was looking over my shoulder when the rule changes were made, and I had no option except being honorably discharged at rank without further reserve commitment.

Chapter VIII

ACCOUNTING PRACTICE

After separation from the Marines, we returned to Snyder in December 1954 to resume my accounting practice and to complete the experience requirement to sit for the final practice section of the CPA exam. I had decided to delay going to law school until the summer session of 1955, which would give more than enough practice time to qualify. Again I would work under the supervision of my dad's partner, Russell Yorgesen, and a new partner, Charles Blakey.

We bought a small house on the outskirts of Snyder, even though we would be leaving Snyder to enroll in law school in about nine months. The plan was to develop some equity, and rent it while at law school. At this point in time, it was possible that after law school I would return and enter the accounting practice with my dad and his partners, having guarded against the peril of losing the tax practice to the lawyers by becoming one. Without further comment, it suffices to say that everyone knows what can happen to the best laid plans.

Work was fairly smooth for the first several months since audit season usually did not start up until the fall and income tax season came thereafter. At that time, tax returns were generally due on March 15 of each year. In the meantime, the firm supervised the in-house accounting of a number of local businesses, prepared quarterly income tax estimates, did a few audits for clients whose fiscal year ended at a time other than December 31 and researched tax questions that clients would inquire about from time to time. If things were slow, I soon learned to disappear with Russell and Charlie to a nearby pool hall. Before my tenure with the firm ended, I am not so sure that my proficiency in *8-ball* and particularly *Snooker* did not exceed my proficiency in accounting matters.

My first serious assignment was to assist in the audit of a governmental client whose accounting fiscal year ended in early fall. We were well into the audit about thirty days when I started work in a department of that entity that assessed and collected taxes. After a few days of reviewing routine records of that department, I felt that the head of the department, who was the father of one of my high school classmates, was noticeably uneasy with my presence. I made a mental note that there were a number of things that he personally handled that involved cash or the equivalent of cash. It's always amazed me how much you can learn from body language and the like. The department head came from a well known local family and I had no reason to suspect that he was anything but completely honest. Still working routinely with tax assessments and collections, I first found a problem with the fact that I noticed working down the assessment lists alphabetically that one of his relative's homes had not been assessed, nor sent a tax bill for the year nor had the tax on his home been paid. Routine was set aside and I checked the tax roll for his personal taxes and his other relatives that I knew. In all of such cases, I either found that there was no assessment and payment, or as more commonly the case, that the taxes were assessed but were to be paid in two installments. The first payments were paid by the relatives when all taxes became due; however, the second payments were never received when due. Furthermore, for several years back, the unpaid balances were not added to the delinquent tax rolls when customarily the delinquent taxes of others had been.

I reported my preliminary findings to Russell and Charlie, and they sent me back with some additional areas to check due to what we had found up to that point. After finding a number of other questionable things, Russell and I met with the department head and he admitted to wrongdoing. Russell then reported his findings to the appropriate authorities of this governmental unit, and the department head was allowed to resign. No criminal proceedings were initiated. Of course, I felt very bad that I had to stumble on this discrepancy on my very first audit, particularly because I knew the family so well. I did realize that this was my job, we were paid to do it and the client relied on us. Nevertheless, the experience chilled my appetite for audit work as this situation was very close and personal. I could also foresee that in a small town the situation might repeat itself, since at that time I am reasonably sure that I knew most of the families who resided there.

After working on several other audit assignments that fall, we next turned to tax work for which my dad had shaped my life to protect. Through March 15 of 1955, we worked like Trojans from early every morning (except Sunday of course) until midnight or later each night. I well remember that we kept all returns to be prepared in rolling file cabinets beside each person's desk. It seemed that every time I worked my files to a reasonable level, someone (usually my dad since he and his brother, Tommy, were heavily involved in their insurance agency) added a bunch more. Now, I was developing serious doubts about this valuable practice that it was my destiny to protect. After one complete tax season, I couldn't possibly envision doing this the rest of my life. Another thought also struck me; why would the lawyers want to take away this drudgery from the accountants who seemed to delight in it. Since I was working for a small salary and did not participate in the partnership profits, I later decided that I probably did not have a complete picture of the rewards. Additionally, I also realized that these were the days before really substantial accounting fees for complex audit work and management services for public companies blossomed; and I have since seen times that the accountants were doing better financially, generally speaking, than the lawyers. Unfortunately perhaps, some of the large accounting firms became too fee dependent upon management services without separating or otherwise insulating their audit responsibilities. We all know the resulting conflicts of interest that did serious economic and legal damage to some of those firms who were involved with corporate clients charged with corruption. Needless to say, the pendulum swings just so far one way until it comes back to the other.

All of this discussion leads to the fact that by the time the fall of 1955 rolled around, I was more than ready to pack up and leave for Austin to see if the grass was greener on the law side; and if so, the chances were slim that I would ever return full time to the accounting side of my education and experience. As it turned out, I never returned to the accounting practice, in Snyder or anywhere else. I did not even complete my CPA requirements. However, my accounting education and experience was not a waste by any means. I drew upon it numerous times during my law practice; and, later in business, I used it on a daily basis and much more frequently than I did my law background.

Chapter IX

UT LAW SCHOOL

My first day at the University of Texas Law School in Austin in the fall of 1955 was interesting in a number of ways. We later were told that registration revealed that the average age of our freshman law class was twenty-seven years, and that was understandable considering the large number of veterans that were enrolling following the Korean conflict. We were also the largest freshman class in the school's long history. As I was walking to the main entrance on that day, the first person I bumped into was a very good undergraduate friend, Taylor Nichols, who had been a fellow fraternity brother. We caught up on each other's military service, as neither of us had heard from the other during that period of time. It turned out that Taylor had entered the air force and had married his old girlfriend from Harlingen, Texas. We then stood in a long line to register and had an extended visit about old times and what a coincidence it was that we were both entering law school at the same time.

We were in line behind a young man who had not been in the service. He volunteered that he had spent the summer preparing for law school by outlining the Texas Law Digest. This was a set of reference books that attempted to incorporate all the case law in Texas within its multiple volume perimeters. He asked what we had done to prepare ourselves for this new undertaking. Both Taylor and I were speechless, as it had not occurred to either of us that we needed to learn all the law in Texas before coming to law school. He was truly amazed about our lack of preparation, and assured us that we would likely find ourselves in the normal fifty percent first-year law school casualty rate. We did not know until later in the day during a speech by Dean Page Keeton that there was actually that high of percentage of first-year failures and dropouts. I believe the dean's statement was to the effect that we should look to the persons to our right and left, and that one of them wouldn't be here at the beginning of our midlaw year. Since Taylor and I were sitting together in the auditorium during the dean's welcoming speech, we were both understandably shaken when we realized that each one of us was either to the right or left of the other. The dean's statement seemed to confirm the casualty rate voiced by the student in the registration line who chastised us for our lack of due diligence in preparing for our first year in law school. Worse still, this made him more of a prophet relative to the wisdom of his outlining all the Texas law before school even started. I do not believe that Taylor got any more sleep than I did that night before we commenced classes the next day. Since the first-year law course study was fairly standard, we had several common classes; however, Taylor elected to take torts from Leon Green, a former dean, and I elected to take the course from Dean Keeton.

At this point, I might add that the law school had a remarkable faculty and physical plant in place. The school has long been one of the outstanding law institutions in the country, largely due to its outstanding faculty. At this time, besides Keeton and Green, both outstanding authorities on the law of torts, the faculty included Charles T. McCormick, evidence; Joseph T. Sneed and John F. Sutton, contracts; Robert W. Stayton, appellate procedure; William F. Fritz and Corwin W. Johnson, property; Gus M. Hodges and E. Wayne Thode, procedure; Jerre S. Williams, Joseph Witherspoon and Charles Alan Wright, constitutional law; George W. Stumberg, conflicts of law and criminal law; Parker Fielder and J. Henry Wilkinson, taxation; William O. Huie and M. K. Woodward, oil and gas; Buck Bailey, wills and trusts; and Pierre R. Loiseaux, labor law and creditor's rights. Many of these faculty members had authored textbooks used in law schools around the country. National surveys, including *The Princeton Review*, have over the years listed Texas as one of the top-ten teaching facilities in the nation. The quality of the faculty was also reflected by the fact that students from all over were coming to the Texas law school. It looked like competition would be tough, since we had a significant number of undergraduates from Harvard, Yale, Princeton, Stamford, Rice and even several Rhodes scholars, not to slight those who came from other prestigious schools not specifically mentioned.

During my first semester in torts, Dean Keeton announced that he was giving a midsemester test. It seems that this was highly usual because most professors who simply let you live or die scholastically with only the final semester exam. You could cut the tension in the class with a knife, since it was quite early in the game and most students were still adjusting to the case method of teaching used at the law school. In short, professors used textbooks which contained actual cases which were read as homework and the professor in the classroom would call on students to recite on the facts and rulings in the assigned cases. The class would then try to develop a rule of law or a group of rules from individual cases and others collected in the same chapter or section of the textbook. Some of the professors aided in the process more than others did. A few left it to each student to do his or her own summary of any particular series of cases. Dean Keeton, however, would give periodic summaries of cases covered and helped the students to organize the applicable principles of law he desired they learn from each section of the casebook. In any event, the class talked a lot among themselves as to how best to study for their first law school exam. A student sitting next to me suggested that two heads are better than one, and that we could study for the exam together. His recitations and comments had seemed fairly much on target to me, so I accepted his offer. We had several study sessions before the exam at my house, which I had bought in the Tarrytown area of Austin with the help of the GI bill's low interest rates. I noticed that we had somewhat different ideas about what was important and what was not.

Exam day came and we struggled. A few days later, we received our test scores and I was horrified that my score was a 59. My study partner was in worse shape with a 38. Knowing nothing else at the time, I resolved in my own mind that I would never study for exams with someone again. I had never done that before in my life with the exception of the business law exam Johnny Allred and I had taken in undergraduate school. I later found out that my score was second highest in the class, but I still felt it was best to study alone in the future. It turned out that this was the dean's way of giving his first year students a wake up call. He also told us that his grading system was based fifty percent on finding and defining the *problem*; and anything over fifty percent was based on what type of *analysis and solution* was suggested in your answer.

Taylor and I had both signed up for Charles Alan Wright's constitutional law class. He was definitely an Ivy League type and a lot different than Dean Keeton. Even then, before his involvement in Watergate, he had a national reputation and was also an authority on evidence. As we were seated in the classroom, he walked to the blackboard and drew a small circle on it. Before saying anything, he faced the blackboard and placed his nose in the circle. He then started his introduction to con law by saying that the subject wasn't good for anything except social talk at cocktail parties. He then assigned one hundred plus pages in the casebook to read before the next class session, and with his nose still implanted in the circle, he dismissed the class early for no stated reason. Taylor and I looked at each other, nodded in agreement and marched straight to the registrar's office to drop the course.

Fortunately, Jerre Williams was teaching another con law class that semester; and since space was available, we eagerly signed up for it. Later, I found Professor Wright to be talented in coaching the *Legal Eagles*, an intramural football team. He was a very good coach and his teams from year to year always placed near the top in intramural football. I would far rather be a student of his in football than one studying con law for cocktail parties.

During the semester, I acquired a home job by a chance meeting with one of my neighbors. He was in the advertising business in Austin and needed someone to do his bookkeeping and prepare a monthly statement. We agreed on a generous monthly salary, which helped pay the bills, along with help from the GI bill and landing a teaching instructor's position for the next semester at the Texas business school. Later, I picked up another set of books to keep, as well as receiving a teaching quizmaster's position for my midlaw year. With no time to spend money, I never had it better financially. The two-bedroom cottage I had purchased was located on a cul-de-sac at the foot of Tower Drive, so named because it was on the downward slope of a hill facing the main tower of the University of Texas which was clearly visible to anyone looking down the street. Except for the cottages on the cul-de-sac, the other houses on Tower Drive up the hill were substantial and definitely one of Austin's *high rent* areas. I had paid $12,000 for the cottage, enjoyed a low payment of about $89 a month for the three years I was in law school; and then sold it upon graduation for $20,000 and some change. I have had a love affair for real estate ever since.

Economics aside, I completed the first year of law school with a grade point average of 86+ on a grading scale that 85 equaled an *A*. This put me within the top five or six in my class. I felt sorry for the student I studied with for Dean Keeton's torts first midsemester test as he was on the first year's fifty percent casualty list. Later I learned he did graduate after having invested five years in a three-year effort.

Another casualty was the guy in the registration line who had already learned all the Texas law by outlining it before coming to law school. Not only was he a first-year casualty, but one that never did graduate after three or four attempts. In any event, the first year's hard work put me in good academic position; and during the second semester I was elected a member of *Phi Delta Phi*, a national honorary legal fraternity and a candidate for the *Texas Law Review*. One of the members of the law review at that time was James A. Baker III, who pursued not only a legal career, but also a political one, highlighted by his appointment as Secretary of State by President George P. Bush.

It also opened a lot of doors for my second year at law school. I was named a teaching quizmaster and was requested by Dean Keeton to write an article on "*An Approach to the Study of Law*" for a law school publication. For whatever it may be worth to anyone interested in studying law, I am including a copy of that article in the appendix to this book. Nearly fifty years have passed since writing that article; I have had many law graduates of the Texas law school either send me a copy of that article or otherwise tell me they had benefited from it. I have no idea if it is still in circulation at the law school. Taylor also did well the first year and was named a student assistant to Dean Page Keeton for the midlaw year and was also elected to membership in *Phi Delta Phi*. Not too bad for two small-town guys who had been subject to a terrorist attack in the registration line the first day at law school.

My midlaw year at law school was very enjoyable, and I now knew beyond a shadow of a doubt that law would be my chosen profession and had told my dad who was not surprised by this time. I was fascinated with the competition within each law class and by the fact that it did not have any adverse effect on friendships between those competing for grades or top honors. Much later, I would find the same was true with practicing lawyers who oppose each other during the day as adversaries, and then socialize by night as friends.

I enjoyed being a quizmaster during my second year, which ordinarily is more recognition than work. However, during the second semester, Professor Henry Wilkinson, to whom I was assigned became ill and could not teach his classes in oil and gas taxation and legal accounting for six to eight weeks. He and the dean asked if I could possibly teach the classes until a substitute could be found. Having taught the business law class in the undergraduate class for a semester, I felt I could handle it, but I did have some reservation due to the fact that this would involve teaching a number of my peers. In any event, it worked out fine and I was not replaced until the professor returned to his teaching duties almost two months later. All things considered, it was a good experience.

During my second year, I wrote two case notes for the *Texas Law Review*. The editorial process is more demanding than the actual writing of the note itself. Initially, it is reviewed by one of the student editors to whom a candidate is assigned. Normally, there are a number of drafts required to get his or her approval. Then the case note is reviewed by a faculty member with skills in the area of the law involving the case about which you are writing. Once again I was fortunate to have one of my midlaw case notes reviewed by Dean Keeton. The note dealt with a case entitled, *Biggers v. Continental Bus System*, and it involved one of Dean Keeton's favorite subjects taught in his torts class, an element of an action for negligent conduct known as *proximate cause*. In a case involving alleged negligence, not only does the plaintiff have to prove conduct or an omission that a jury decides meets the court's definition of negligence but also that such conduct was the proximate cause of the accident and/or injury that resulted in the suit. Essentially, this is a causation issue. Former Dean Green would leave it at that; however, Dean Keeton went a lot further in his interpretation of the *proximate* part of the causation definition. In layman's terms, it is easy to view causation when a driver runs a red light and strikes the plaintiff's automobile resulting in a broken limb for example.

However, one can stretch causation so far that it is not proximate; e.g., it is also true that the accident would not have happened if the defendant had not awaken the morning of the accident, simply because he would not have been at the site of the accident. The stretch between the two examples is what the word *proximate* has to do with causation. In the bus case I reviewed for my case note, on a slippery road a driver rear-ended the plaintiff's car, propelling it diagonally in front of an oncoming bus. The jury found the bus driver guilty of failing to keep a proper lookout and driving at an unlawful speed. A court of appeals reversed the verdict against the bus company, stating as a matter of law that the negligence of the bus driver was not a proximate cause of the collision. The Supreme Court of Texas affirmed the court of appeals' decision relieving the bus company from responsibility. The majority of both appellate courts stated that the two elements of proximate cause were causation and foreseeability, and concluded that foreseeability was completely lacking because it was not usual and customary for a car to be hit and propelled into the wrong lane of traffic. Thus, they were saying that the injury to the plaintiff could not have been reasonably foreseen by the negligent bus driver hitting a car which had suddenly been propelled in front of it. It was too remote in terms of the stretch of the *foreseeability* concept between my example of the bus driver not waking up that morning and the ability to foresee that another driver's conduct in striking the plaintiff's car first could activate the bus driver's negligence in driving too fast and not keeping a proper lookout.

Dean Keeton felt the case was wrongly decided and that the resulting injury could have been reasonably foreseen as a result of the negligent bus driver, which was also my conclusion in the case note. When my case note was still in draft form awaiting the Dean's approval to publish, it somehow found its way into the hands of one of the Supreme Court's justices; and it was then circulated in some fashion among the other justices on the court. It so happened that the plaintiff's attorney had filed a motion for a rehearing with the court that was still pending. I found out about the situation when I received a call from the plaintiff's attorney who told me that the defense attorney had raised cane about an unpublished case note of the *Texas Law Review* floating around the court's chambers during oral arguments on the motion for the rehearing. The plaintiff's attorney wanted a copy of the draft. There was nothing wrong with the court's consideration of a law review article, comment or case note; and such sources are often considered. What was unusual was the fact that an unpublished note would find its way into the court's chambers in the first place; and that either a justice or staff member in the court had in some manner advised the defense lawyer of its existence in an ex parte communication of some type in other than open court. In any event, my case note was published shortly thereafter. The Supreme Court reversed the case on rehearing and the plaintiff was awarded the substantial damages the jury had awarded. My ego trip was that the court's reasoning followed substantially the argument I had advanced in the case note, which had been supervised by the dean of the law school. Little did I realize at the time that the *Biggers* decision would sometimes be troublesome for me down the line when my trial work was nearly always on the defense side of the bar.

During January of that year, my oldest son, Lyle, was born the night before my final exam in trusts. I spend most of the evening in the lobby of the delivery room attempting to review my notes for the next morning's exam. I was so exhausted during the exam that I had little idea the next day as to what questions were asked, much less what my answers had been. I had attached a cigar to my exam paper which announced my son's birth and to give the professor some clue as to why my exam paper might seem somewhat disorientated, more so than usual as I had taken a course under the same professor before. I do not know if the message helped, but the professor posted a grade of 86 for me in the course.

As the midlaw year came to a close, once again I was amply rewarded for effort expended. First off, I was elected by my peers on the editorial board of the *Texas Law Review* to be its comment editor for my senior year. I had maintained my position in the top-five students academically. I was chosen by the faculty and my fellow students as the *Outstanding Midlaw Student* for the year and received such recognition during the annual *Law Day* ceremonies. This was a very special day attended by the faculty, students, dignitaries and a nationally known speaker. In addition, it was more than just glory and honor for awardees since the leading law firms in the state provided cash awards to go along with the certificates of recognition. In my case, I received a $100 check from *Baker & Botts*, in Houston, Texas, which provided me with a much-needed new suit of clothes. Believe it or not, you could buy a very nice suit for that amount of money in the fifties. I was also elected president of Phi Delta Phi, my legal fraternity for the next year.

During the first semester of my senior year, everything was under control and going smoothly. I had my hands full as a quizmaster and comment editor of the law review. About the only time that serious law students relax is by going to the Texas football games in Austin, some participation in intramural sports and occasional bridge games on Saturday nights. One couple we knew usually hosted these bridge games. There was only one drawback. The wife always prepared more coffee than needed the morning of a bridge game, left it sitting in the pot all day and reheated it for her guests to *enjoy* that evening. The coffee was so strong that you could hardly pour it, much less stir it without breaking the spoon. The caffeine lasted all the next week and it was not a problem staying awake late at nights to study. At least, I think that was the proximate cause of the matter.

The other activity that ate up a lot of time during the first semester of my senior year was employment interviews. Of course, this is what it is all about. In all, I interviewed ten firms; four of the top firms in Houston, three of the large Dallas firms, the largest firm in Denver and one of the best-known firms in Washington, DC. In all cases, either I was offered a job or there was indication that if I were to call back to the firm after returning home, I would probably receive an offer. That latter situation was a game a number of the prestigious firms around the country used—that is, to have the student affirmatively let them know they wanted to work for them before extending an offer. Otherwise, they must have felt it would be a blow to their collective egos to risk having their job offer turned down. One will notice that so far I have only listed nine firms in Houston, Dallas, Denver and Washington, DC, but I said I interviewed a total of ten. The tenth interview came late in November when I thought I was through with the process. I had narrowed the field to two firms, one of which was Fulbright, Crooker, Freeman, Bates & Jaworski in Houston. Fulbright had not only opened their financial books to me but had also made the most interesting offer. They wanted me to work with their trial section, as well as their taxation section, for several years with a view to establishing a new *tax litigation department* in their firm. As it was, in order to try a tax case, they were using one trial attorney working with one tax attorney. Kraft Eidman and Newton Gresham of that firm had also requested that I not accept any employment from any other firm without first returning to Houston and talking further with them. Well, I agreed since I admired their openness and saw their offer as a possible way to advance to partnership status sooner than normally was possible with the big firms—anywhere from seven to fifteen years normally with *never* as a third possibility. We tentatively agreed on a return to the firm by Thanksgiving if I were considering any other firm but them.

The tenth firm interview occurred shortly before Thanksgiving. It did not originate in the normal way via the student employment office or posted notice that a firm was planning to interview. Instead, I got a call at home from Dean

Keeton advising me that he wanted to see me in a suit and tie at his office at 2 PM that day for an interview. I told him I was done with interviews and close to having to make a decision soon. He advised me that first and foremost I was interviewing that afternoon, but that I was under no obligation to do anything but hear out the firm's representative. I would have done nearly anything for the dean as we had become friends over the past few years. I dutifully appeared as summoned. He introduced me to Thornton Hardie from El Paso. My first thought was a vision of my stay there in the bed of a murdered husband and being one of only three marines at Fort Bliss! I didn't think this interview would go far, even though I knew that Thornton Hardie was the chairman of the Board of Regents of the University of Texas. He was a fine old gentleman with silver hair and tongue, and he told me all the advantages of living in a place like El Paso, near the ski and golf resorts of Ruidosa and Cloudcroft, New Mexico. He also told me that El Paso was the number-one ranked city in Texas for lawyers' earnings on a per capita basis. He offered to show me the firm's books if I would come that weekend to El Paso for an interview with his firm, then Hardie, Grambling, Sims & Galatzan. Among other clients, he said they represented a number of banks in El Paso and served as the general attorney for El Paso Natural Gas Company, the city's most significant employer. In fact, their offices occupied the third floor of the gas company building. I thanked him for the information and told him I would let him know if I had any interest in going to El Paso for an interview that weekend or any other. However, he preferred the coming weekend because he was going to have a big party at his house and many of the firm's clients would be there. In any event, the dean seemed grateful that I did not turn him down on the spot.

I decided before the weekend that I needed to make the trip. Several things he said were interesting. I could look at their books and compare the per capita results with Fulbright's.

He mentioned that everyone who came to the firm had to try cases for at least three years. Even if they became transactional lawyers, they would have the benefit, in drafting documents, of knowing that a jury can make its own interpretation of the instrument if the draftsman leaves any ambiguity in it. He also had mentioned that normally if a new attorney had the right stuff, the firm would advance him or her from associate to partner status in three or four years. So I went to El Paso that weekend and was charmed by everyone I met and by the numbers in the firm's books for the last three years or so. The firm had only nine attorneys at the time, and I liked every one of them. I was hooked, but I told Mr. Hardie that I could not accept employment until I kept my promise to Fulbright at Thanksgiving.

This was not an easy obligation to face, particularly when I had to tell them I had decided to accept employment in El Paso. When I met with Newton Gresham and Kraft Eidman in Houston, they were very disappointed, but quite gracious when I told them. They let me know after lunch that if anything went wrong in El Paso, I would have a home in Houston with their firm. I called Mr. Hardie in El Paso as soon as I returned to Austin and accepted employment. With the job after graduation handled, I could get back to my law school activities.

Studies continued to go well, except Taylor Nichols and I had deliberately been postponing taking Creditors' Rights, as it had a reputation of being the most boring course in law school. Finally, we caved and signed up for the course. It proved to deserve its reputation. We started to cut classes regularly to preserve our sanity and to get our other chores done. Taylor continued as student assistant to the dean, and I had my law review and quizmaster work, not to mention keeping books and preparing financial statements for my two accounting clients at home. At this point of time, the law school had no attendance rule. Their position was that a student was only cutting his or her own throat by cutting class.

With final exams for the course in sight, I had a plan. The girl who sat next to me when I did go to the class was some type of stenographer or the like before coming to law school. She took all her notes in shorthand and had told me on several occasions that she daily typed her class notes from the short hand. She had also told me that I was welcome to have a copy of her typed notes since I was absent so much. I told Taylor not to worry; that I would be happy to make him a copy. About four days before the exam, I asked her for a full copy of her typed notes for the semester, which she willingly provided. Without reading them at the time, I made a copy for Taylor. I normally reviewed my notes the night before the exam. On that night, I sat down and pulled out her notes that were neatly typed. I read the first few pages and decided she was from Venus and I from Mars. Nothing made any sense to me, and I decided that she must have been smoking something when she transcribed her notes from shorthand. This assumed that she knew what she was writing down in the first place. Anyway, I had no sooner panicked than I received a telephone call from Taylor. Great minds run in the same direction, I guess, since he had independently arrived at the same conclusion: what to do? I then remembered that a friend of mine from El Paso had taken this course the summer before at the University of Colorado law school, and his professor was the one who had written our textbook. I called my friend, Fred Morton, immediately and asked him if he had retained his notes from this class. Somebody was looking out for drunks, idiots and wayward law students that night as Fred had the notes in his possession. I got in the car and went to Fred's apartment to pick them up. I called Taylor to meet me at my house and we would go over them jointly because we didn't have time to have them copied. He did, and we did. This broke my long-standing rule of not studying with anybody for law school exams. We had no choice and worked until the late morning hours reviewing the notes. For the first time since the course started, it made some sense.

We took the exam the next morning and both made a passing grade. However, it was the lowest grade I made in three years at the law school—a 75 (or a B under an alpha grading system). I was embarrassed, but knew I deserved it by violating my study habits for the first time in law school. Also for the first time, I decided to request a review of my paper by the professor, which was a fairly common procedure at the time. I met with him and he let me know that he was very disappointed in my performance in his class and particularly with my attendance. I gave him all kind of excuses, but we both knew I was guilty as charged. And he did, however, review the paper and its grade. Several minutes into the review of the multiple choice portion of the exam, he discovered that he had used the wrong template to grade it. The template was one he had used in a similar exam in the same course, but with variations of the questions asked. He now was as embarrassed as I was for my poor performance. The review would have improved my grade to about 81. Since I had so many grades under my belt over three years, we determined that neither the lower or higher score would significantly affect my overall grade point average. I suggested that he leave it alone as it was a big deal for a professor to change posted grades. However, I did suggest that if anyone had failed the course, he review his or her paper to see if they would have passed had the proper template been used. He agreed, and fortunately there was only one student in the failing category whose grade had to be raised and reported to the dean's office in order that the student would pass the course. At least, I felt that some good came out of my attempt to improve my score, when I knew deep down that I did not deserve any consideration due to my poor classroom attendance.

Late each semester of each year, the *Chancellors*, a local law school honorary society selected the six top students in the senior class, considering grades and other contributions to the law school. This ceremony is one of the most colorful events during the law school year. Old members enter the classroom after three loud knocks on the door, *tap* the new members, place black hoods over their heads and then lead them out of the classroom. When all six new members have been *tapped*, the group is then shackled with a heavy rope around all their necks and they are led around the school carrying heavy books. Once out of sight, in a private area, the group is initiated and informed of their offices for the next year. The offices, in order of prestige, are *grand chancellor*, *vice-chancellor*, *clerk*, *keeper of the peregrinus* and two *chancellors-at-large*. My day came and I was selected and designated the *clerk* of my group.

During the last semester of school my senior year, the dean appointed Taylor and me to be cochairmen of the Speakers Committee for Law Day. This in itself was a high honor as we would help with the selection of outstanding speakers for that event and make all the arrangements for their attendance. The speakers we selected were U.S. Secretary of the Treasury, Robert B. Anderson, for the keynote, and as additional speakers,Illinois Supreme Court Justice Walter V. Schaefer and Texas Supreme Court Justice St. John Garwood. The contact with these three outstanding lawyers was stimulating to say the least. We had a great Law Day celebration that everyone connected to the law school attends. This country boy was lucky once more to receive awards, and was recognized as the *Senior Student Whose Character and Ability Give the Greatest Promise of Achieving Distinction in the Practice of Law* and the *Phi Delta Phi Graduate of the Year*. In addition, I was awarded a *Consul Award*, which was very meaningful for me. This selection is for the law students who have made the most outstanding contributions to the law school through their active participation in extracurricular activities. It is made by a committee which reflects the viewpoints of a wide cross section of the student body and whose members are individually familiar with law school activities and the students participating in them. The most promising senior award also brought another $100 check, this time from the Houston firm of *Andrews, Kurth, Campbell & Bradley*; and so I was able to buy my second suit in two years and in time to be well dressed to commence the practice of law.

I soon learned that my designation as Phi Delta Phi Graduate of theYear carried with it consideration for the national fraternity's *Graduate of the Year* program. Letters of recommendation were written on my behalf by Dean Keeton and Newton Gresham of Fulbright, Crooker, Freeman, Bates & Jaworski of Houston. When the national results were announced, the committee, which included practicing attorneys, judges and law professors from around the country, stated that the balloting was exceptionally close, resulting in a virtual tie among four candidates. The winner was from Illinois and I was happy to have been in the running and to be the graduate of the year for the southern region of the United States.

My final act as president of the local chapter of Phi Delta Phi came when it was time for us to initiate some prominent lawyer or judge as an honorary member during our final social meeting of the year. We decided that it would be held at the Austin Country Club. My friend from El Paso, Fred Morton, who gave me his notes on Creditors' Rights just happened to have grown up next door to Judge R. E. Thomason, the then presiding federal judge sitting in El Paso. We decided that we should nominate him to be our honorary member for the local chapter that year. Taylor Nichols agreed as he also accepted a job offer in El Paso. The chapter accepted and we invited him to be with us at our annual banquet. A great time was had by all, and I was able to spend some quality time getting to know the federal judge before whom I hoped to practice soon in El Paso. At this point, I disclaim any benefit from the old saying that a "good lawyer knows the law but that a great lawyer knows the judge." A last word on that subject, Fred Morton was going to El Paso to clerk for Judge Thomason.

Finally, graduation came and the great adventure of law school came to its conclusion. I was selected to membership in the *Order of the Coif*, a national honorary society and graduated *summa cum laude* with my bachelor of law degree, later converted by name change to doctor of jurisprudence.

Chapter X

LAW PRACTICE—LITIGATION YEARS

Upon arriving in El Paso during the summer of 1958 to commence my law practice, the first order of business was to purchase a home. The first decision was to decide on the area of the city we wanted to live. All the partners and associates of the firm lived on the west side of El Paso, and they assured me that it was probably my best choice. El Paso physically sits on the north bank of the Rio Grande River, separating it from Mexico, and extends on both sides of the foothills of the Franklin Mountains, which generally lay in a northerly direction from the river. Downtown is virtually at the foot of the mountain range and residential areas are generally divided into the west and the east sides of the mountain. All the military reservations, at that time Biggs Air Force and Fort Bliss army bases, were located on the east side. On the east side, the soil is sandy in consistency; and on the west side, the soil is just a top coat for the rocky substrata beneath. Accordingly, the west side homes were somewhat more expensive to build than the same house on the east side because of the extra labor and costs in the foundation. However, from the west side, you have a more direct route to downtown and less traffic.

Thus, I agreed with my firm members' advice to locate on the west side of El Paso. Following a brief survey, I found that a new house could generally be purchased at $10 per square foot. Accordingly, we purchased a 1600-square-foot house for $16,000. This three-bedroom house seemed adequate for two adults and two small children. My next project was to get rid of my gas-guzzling 1953 Lincoln which I had purchased in Fredericksburg, Virginia, from a retired naval officer who had a Lincoln-Mercury dealership and had the reputation of giving naval and marine officers a good deal. I drove it on to a Ford's dealer's used car lot as it was almost ready to drop dead. I finally worked out a trade on a 1957 Ford sedan with low mileage, an overdrive standard transmission and no air-conditioning. Having spent several months in El Paso at Fort Bliss, I knew this car would be hot; but I rationalized that most of my time the first few years would be spent working, and I could survive the heat until I could afford something better and air-conditioned. Besides, factory-installed air-conditioning in cars was still rather new, and after-market installations sucked. I knew, as I had one installed on my old Lincoln in Lubbock, Texas. Just when you needed it, the air conditioner compressor would freeze and you were done until you stopped and let the build up of ice melt.

I next reported for work at the firm and was assigned a small office that had been acquired for me but was located in the hall just outside of the law firm's existing space. It mattered not, since it was unlikely that I would be entertaining any clients of my own for a while. In the meantime, it was all I could do to see over the top of my desk, since every lawyer in the firm used it to dump research and other projects for me to do. I found that the input of work each day was close to the amount of work that I was able to accomplish during a ten to twelve hour day. Initially, I had planned to be the first person to arrive at work, but Thornton Hardie always seemed to beat me. After a week or so of early arrival, he called me into his office and told me the story of when he joined the firm some fifty years before. At that time, the partners of the firm were two brothers, named Jones. One was a real estate lawyer and one was a litigator. The real estate guy, Cyrus Jones, was always there before Thornton Hardie arrived, no matter at what hour. Mr. Hardie told me that he played this game until he arrived at 4:00 AM one day and Cyrus Jones was there. After that he told me he came to work at whatever time suited him. He advised me to do the same, as no one could do effective work without a good night's sleep and some reasonable time for relaxation. I doubt that if I had accepted employment by any of the big firms in Houston, Dallas, Denver or Washington, I would have received the same advice assuming anyone was there to notice my arrival time.

Of course, when I first arrived in El Paso the results of the bar examination had not been received. Therefore, I knew it was going to be about three months before I would know the results. Without a license to practice law, I realized that for the present I was nothing more than a clerk in the firm. Then the horrible thought hit me square between the eyes what would happen if I failed to pass the exam? Those guys from St. Mary's at the bar exam had worried me. I wondered if any graduate *summa cum laude* of the Texas law school had ever been hired by its chairman of its Board of Regents and then flunked the examination to practice law. The thought was too devastating to harbor and I dismissed it from my mind. However, if it happened, it would be a story that could haunt a person for the rest of their life. In September, when the grades were available, a great burden was lifted from my shoulders when I was notified that I had passed with room to spare.

At this point, I was soon given a very meaningful assignment from "Judge" Morris Galatzan, one of the named partners of the firm who at one time had sat as a state court district judge before coming with the firm. He asked me to help him with the defense of the El Paso Water Improvement District No. 1 of El Paso County in a case involving a lot of money and brought against them by a Houston highway contractor. He wanted me to prepare the answer after a preliminary interview the general manager of the district and its consulting engineer. The dispute involved the type of pavement required to be replaced when the contractor had to cut through an existing roadway to lay water pipe in the city or county. These existing surfaces were either some type of asphalt or concrete pavement. The controversy involved the asphalt surfaces, which were of two types: (1) inverted penetration pavement; and (2) hot or cold mix asphalt pavement. The two varieties of asphalt surfaces are composed of essentially the same materials, i.e., oil asphalt and crushed rock particles. They differ, however, in that the ingredients of inverted penetration pavement are not premixed prior to its application, but are applied by spreading the oil asphalt on top of crushed gravel first placed on the roadway. There is a tremendous cost difference between the two processes, the premixed process being much more expensive. To compound matters, the detailed contract prepared by the water district from language furnished by their consulting engineer had detailed specifications that described the exact way that "asphalt pavement" had to be prepared and the manner and contents of the mix. As it turned out, this description would have been sufficient for most high traffic freeways.

The contractor, however, found mostly inverted penetration pavement existing on the roads and streets he cut. He relied on a statement in the bid proposal where the contractor is to insert his quantity and price bid on the job, and this general description stated it was for "repairing and/or replacing paving in kind and type, the sum of $______." Without apparently reading the detailed provisions of the contract where "asphalt pavement" was discussed, he took the quoted language to mean he could replace a cut in asphalt pavement with exactly the same type as he had cut. He had talked with the general manager of the water district, who when shown the quoted language by the contractor, apparently agreed with his interpretation that he could replace exactly what he found. When he had repaved the first couple of cuts, the engineer told him that was not what the contract called for and that it must be done in accordance with the detailed specifications of the agreement, i.e., asphalt pavement mixed and contented for substantial highways. This would leave the cut better than the rest of the road repaired. The engineer maintained cuts need to be better to stand up to future wear and tear. Rather than gamble on the outcome then and walk off the job, the contractor repaired all asphalt roads with the super mix as opposed to the kind and type that he found on the roadway. Upon completion, he sued the water district for the difference in costs and other items of damage, contending they were extra or additional work.

After doing the initial research on the case, I recommended that we file a motion for summary judgment on behalf of our client. Judge Galatzan agreed, although he did not think we would get a summary judgment granted as it was not too popular with the judiciary in those days. Fundamentally, the procedure consists of filing a motion before any trial of the case together with affidavits setting forth the facts which, if undisputed, entitles the moving party to judgment as a matter of law. Typically, the other side files affidavits attempting to prove that fact issues for the jury exist, and therefore the moving party is not entitled to judgment as a matter of law. To me, the rules of construing a written contract in Texas were clear that this agreement was not ambiguous and could be construed from the *four corners* of the contract; and that the oral discussions of the contractor and the district manager of the water district could not be considered in the case because of the parole evidence rule. This rule prohibits the introduction of oral evidence to contradict or vary the terms of an unambiguous contract. Another Texas rule of contract construction is that general provisions cannot be relied upon to vary specific provisions of the contract. Thus, in this case, the general bid proposal language referring to *like kind and type* replacement of road cuts could not alter the detailed unambiguous provisions of the specifications, which said that all streets in the project would be repaved with a like material of either (1) cement concrete pavement with the mix and process specified or (2) asphalt pavement with the mix and process specified, depending on whether concrete or asphalt pavement was cut. Of course, neither of the two choices includes repaving with inverted penetration pavement. Under the detailed specs, if that type of pavement is encountered, it must be replaced with the asphalt pavement as specified since it is not *like* the only other alternative of cement concrete pavement.

Our motion was filed, and in due course, the trial court granted our motion. The plaintiff appealed and the court of appeals agreed with us and affirmed the lower court's decision. The plaintiff did not give up and asked that the Supreme Court of Texas to reverse the court of appeals decision. They refused. The plaintiff added a few more distinguished appellate attorneys to the two sets of attorneys, one from El Paso and one from Houston, who had previously handled the case; and they then filed a second motion for rehearing with the Supreme Court of Texas. After more briefing, ours and theirs, the court refused to reconsider the case, and victory was ours. Lesson to be learned from this case: *any businessman, big or small, who undertakes work pursuant to a written agreement, should have it reviewed by a competent attorney who understands the nuts and bolts of his or her client's business to be certain the scope of the work is completely understood and any ambiguity resolved or removed from it before it is signed.* Since I had handled all the research and briefing at all levels of the controversy, Judge Galatzan made sure all the firm members knew that. I felt that this was a good start for my new career.

I was put under the tutorial wing of John Grambling at this point. He was the leading trial lawyer for the firm, and he and I worked together for the next year or so trying all types of cases. When he felt I was ready, he turned me loose solo and I spent the next eight years doing primarily trial work relating to insurance defense, product liability and medical malpractice defense. I had been well taught, since the bottom line for eight years of intensive trial work was approximately

145 jury cases tried with only two adverse jury decisions. In addition, I tried a number of nonjury cases and settled many others without trial. Like the *gambler*, a lawyer must know when to *hold* and when to *fold*. If the case is a loser, the faster it is disposed of by settlement the less the cost to the client. Said another way, *the first loss is the easiest and problem cases do not get better with age*. We always had lawyers at Monday morning docket call when cases were called and could be set for trial by either side of the case. Usually, only plaintiff lawyers set cases. We set cases that were called when we were on the defense. We moved a lot of cases by settling them for reasonable sums by keeping the heat on the plaintiffs' attorneys who often had more case volume than they could reasonably handle. John Grambling was the architect of this strategy, and it paid off handsomely for our clients.

Of the jury cases I tried, I won quite a few that I shouldn't have. Those were ones I had tried to settle, but for one reason or the other, the plaintiffs' attorneys would not accept a reasonable settlement amount. Unfortunately for their clients, they got nothing instead of something. There is no such thing as a lay-down lawsuit. At least, I have never seen one. A good settlement is better than a good lawsuit in most cases. As a general rule and if I were personally a party, I would rather set the settlement amount than to leave it up to a jury that might turn out unsympathetic or hostile to me for some reason. Ironically, the two jury verdicts that I lost were of two types. The first concerned the representation of a national candy manufacturer, who made a famous nut and chocolate bar. The plaintiff, who was a civil service worker at the local army base in El Paso, claimed the candy bar contained the jawbone of a rat. Biting into it, he caused considerable dental damage and the repair work was done by a dentist at the base. We were in no position to dispute the existence of the jawbone of the rat being in the candy bar, as it had happened to the company on a prior occasion. We were attempting to settle the case for some reasonable sum but were never able to do that. The plaintiff also was requesting large damages due to the fact that he had sustained physiological damages because this candy bar had been his favorite and he could not eat one any longer; thus, he alleged his life was just a shadow of what it had been when he could enjoy the ecstasy of eating his favorite treat. His attorney wanted a minimum of $50,000 for settlement, and I advised the client that we should try the case, admit liability for the occurrence and contest damages only.

On the Monday morning we commenced the trial, I looked over the jury panel and suffered pain when it turned out that almost forty percent of the panel had some connection to either civil service or to the military at Fort Bliss, where the plaintiff was employed and where his dentist was based. I did not have enough challenges to remove all of these persons from the panel without cause. Accordingly, the jury contained five persons who had some common connection with the plaintiff. I learned a valuable lesson from this case: *you cannot judge a book by its cover*. The jury returned a verdict of only $1,000; I had offered $5,000. In talking with jurors afterwards, they told me that they liked the fact that we admitted liability and were only contesting the nondental related claims. The verdict was adverse, but not unfavorable.

The other *loser* was a real disappointment to me. The facts were simple. A big national company had hired a local, small contractor to install a foam process in a number of large trailers my client manufactured and would sell to Safeway Food Company for refrigerated foods. The contractor delivered the first ten units to my client, who refused to accept them because the foam installation was faulty. They had those units examined by a chemist employed by Pacific Car Company, and he was the foremost expert in the field. There were a number of standard tests in the industry for determining quality for this process, and the work of the local installer failed each and every one of them. My client refused to allow the local installer to do any more work on the trailers or attempt to rectify his mistake. They also refused to pay him for the work done on the original ten trailers. The installer sued the national trailer manufacturer in El Paso for the work done on the initial trailers and for lost profits on the balance of the units which were taken away from him and turned over to another installer in California where my client was headquartered.

I was hired to defend the case upon the recommendation of a client of mine who retailed trailers for the national company in El Paso. I examined the files and interviewed the chemist from PacCar, who was probably the most qualified expert I ever encountered. He was not only highly qualified but articulate as well. The client was unwilling to make even a token offer of settlement. I advised the client that there was little doubt that they were in the right, but there were costs to trying the case and that those could be saved if we could make a small but reasonable settlement. They refused because of *principle.* We tried the case. The PacCar chemist was excellent in testifying about the inferior work. During my cross examination of the plaintiff, he testified that he had done prior refrigeration work directly for Safeway and they loved it. During the noon recess, I called and was fortunate to reach the local manager who remembered the work done by the plaintiff for them. His kindest description of the quality of that work is unprintable and he opined that they would never give the plaintiff in our case any more work. He also was willing to, and did, testify that the plaintiff was being less than candid about Safeway being happy with his work. He also testified as to the poor quality of the work without resorting to the more graphic description given me over the telephone.

At the end of the trial and while the jury was out, I reported to my client in California that the outcome looked good as everything in the trial had gone our way. Imagine my surprise a few hours later when the jury wrote a verdict for the plaintiff for about $25,000 for the work done on the ten units he had completed. When I approached the jury after they were released, one older woman started to cry and hugged my neck. She said that she knew that I was disappointed, and she thought I had tried a marvelous case. If so, I asked her why did the jury render even the partial judgment for the installer? She and the other jurors who had then gathered around her then told me that my client was right about quality, but that this *big* national company was wrong not to let the *little* local installer have a chance to fix the problem. So, here in a case where the evidence was clear that the product was crap and the plaintiff was not truthful about Safeway's satisfaction with his work for them, the jury nevertheless felt they had to level the playing field. They decided to pay him for the work done, but not for the loss of profits on the other forty units taken away from him by my client. I learned another valuable lesson for the future: *even if you are right and someone had wronged you, always give the "little guy" a chance to correct his mistake before you trash him, especially if you are a "large corporate type."* I cannot tell you how much this lesson saved me later in life when I had shifted my legal career to a business one.

After I had several years of litigation under my belt, I had an automobile client die in a private airplane crash that he had rented and was piloting from El Paso to Albuquerque, New Mexico. He went down on an Indian reservation that was south of his destination. He had a lawyer friend on board who was injured, but survived the crash. I got a call from the dealer's brother who was one of the co-owners of the dealership. He told me that there was a rumor around the airport that something was wrong with the aircraft he had rented. He wanted me to investigate to see if there was anything to the rumor. I put out word in several directions that I had been hired by the pilot's family to look into matter. The first call I got was from friends of the pilot that had been with him and his passenger at an afternoon party before they left late in the day to go to Albuquerque. They were unhappy that someone was spreading the rumor that the pilot had been drinking that afternoon and this was the probable cause of the crash. They admitted he had at least one drink in the afternoon, but he was not intoxicated when he left the party. The next call was from the passenger, who asked me to come to the hospital and talk. I did, and he related the circumstances of the entire trip until the time of the crash. He said that as it was starting to get dark and when they were less than fifty miles from their destination, the engine just quit. The pilot commenced circling the immediate area to determine the best place for an emergency landing. He decided the nearest roadway in the area was too crowded and that the best available place to land was in a nearby pasture on the Indian reservation. It was completely surrounded by tall trees; some according to the passenger were probably one hundred feet tall. In any event, just as he was making his final approach, all electrical went out on the plane including the front lights just as dusk turned to dark. The plane's wing hit the top several feet of a big tree and cart wheeled into the ground. The engine was driven back into the cockpit killing the pilot. It missed the passenger who survived with a number of injuries. The passenger asked that I represent him if I found there was a basis for suit. I told him that might be possible if we determined there were no conflicts with the pilot's family.

The plane had been rented from a local fixed base operator (FBO), who sold, rented and repaired aircraft. I had found out from other sources that the plane was relatively new, having only been flown about 750 hours. I knew I needed to obtain the maintenance records and flight logs. Without filing a lawsuit, I could only obtain them if the owners of the FBO would voluntarily let me examine them. We commenced a dialogue with them. The owners were two brothers who I knew as I occasionally flew out of their facility with a client who owned his own plane. While talking to them, I got a strange call from a man who claimed he previously worked for the brothers and had information that would be important.

I asked him, "Your place or mine?" He elected to come to my office, and he did. The short hand rendition of what he told me was that although the aircraft that crashed was relatively new, it had engine compression readings recorded during required one hundred hour inspections that were concerning and might have indicated excessive wear. He also said that one of the brothers who owned the FBO had flown this plane just before an inspection was due; and that to avoid doing it, he had turned the tachometer back to read that it had only been flown a total of fifty or sixty hours. He said that the company maintained a daily flight log on each of their airplanes, but they had a fire in their office building between the time of the record alteration and the time the plane crashed. So when the plane went down, the owners were confident that the log had been destroyed, and therefore wouldn't be worried about discovery of the tachometer having been turned back. The company fired this employee after the fire and before the plane crashed. This would be good testimony, but I knew the company would cry a *disgruntled employee* is making this all up. I asked him one more question: "Do you have any type of documentary evidence to support your story?"

I was amazed when he told me he had, and then reached into his jacket and pulled out a charred booklet. It was the internal flight log that he had found after the fire and had decided to keep it since he knew what it would reveal and also knew his employment relationship was rocky at that time. I thought how valuable this log would be if my clients decided they wanted to file a lawsuit, but I was concerned that this guy might want to sell his evidence. Of course, it would be unethical to buy it or his oral testimony. I held my breath when I next asked him if I could have the log book. He handed it to me with a comment that he was happy to put these people in their place.

After conferring with the deceased pilot's brother who was the executor of his estate, he wanted to sue even though the potential damages would probably be affected by the fact that his brother was divorced and his children were not receiving anything other than the court-required child support. He authorized me to proceed and also felt like it would be beneficial to join with the injured passenger, who was a very good personal friend of the family. Suit was filed and months of discovery ensued. I hired the head of the aviation department of the University of Southern California as my expert. We first examined the remains of the aircraft and its engine in the "morgue" for airplanes in Dallas. The FBO which had rented the plane was insured by Lloyds of London; and they hired a very experienced aviation defense lawyer in Dallas, who had defended the "Electra" commercial airplane crash case which had been filed by John Hill, a noted Texas plaintiff attorney and a former governor of the State of Texas. The FBO lawyer, on behalf of his nominal client, brought a third-party action against the airplane manufacturer and the engine manufacturer. This third-party action was brought in our El Paso district court, and it was beginning to look like the courtroom would be very crowded when the case went to trial. Another noted Dallas lawyer filed an answer on behalf of the aircraft manufacturer and still another large firm lawyer from Dallas filed one on behalf of engine manufacturer. The FBO lawyer also filed a second suit against the same third-party defendants in the federal court in Los Angeles, to which we were not a party. This permitted the three defendants in our case to do their discovery in the federal case without our knowledge. In any event, it looked like solvency was not an issue for us and so we concentrated on keeping the heat on the fixed base operators, hoping their attorneys would keep the heat on the plane and engine manufacturer.

Our only involvement in the California case, and actually our first knowledge that it existed, was when the FBO lawyer subpoenaed my USC aircraft expert to testify in that case about two weeks before we were scheduled to go to trial in

El Paso. This was because at that time the Texas rule on expert testimony permitted the opposing party to question the expert hired by the other side about what he had done and about his fact findings. It did not permit the other side to obtain his opinion concerning what he found. In the federal case in California, it appeared that it was likely that they were also entitled to his ultimate opinion. We considered the California case a ruse to keep us in the dark about their discovery, but had no choice but to let our expert appear in response to the subpoena. He asked that I represent him with respect to his deposition.

We appeared and the FBO lawyer quizzed my witness about all his inspections and facts discovered. During our engine inspection, he had found ripples in the cylinder walls, which led him to believe there had been excessive engine wear. His opinion was that this accounted for some of the less than satisfactory compression readings noted on the official engine log for the airplane (as opposed to the internal flight log which had daily not-periodic readings such as the engine log). The engine failed due to the fact that an exhaust valve broke in flight. It was a single engine plane; therefore, it was completely without power. My expert would have testified that there was a bulletin outstanding from the engine manufacturer before the crash that advised the owners of this type of engine to replace the exhaust valves when the next overhaul was required. This plane was not due for a major overhaul for a long time. But my expert would say that his findings indicated unreasonable behavior on the part of the FBO not to give this engine, with its known irregular compression readings, a *top* overhaul. This procedure should be done anytime things do not seem right with an engine. Thus, if the FBO had performed this procedure, they would be mandated by the bulletin to replace all the exhaust valves with somewhat thicker ones. Consequently, he reasoned that the valve would not have broken and the plane crash could have been avoided.

I didn't really care if they got my expert's opinion so close to trial time, but they it created substantial expense to do this in California in what I already felt was a phony case. The FBO lawyer then reached the point in the deposition that he started to ask "opinion" questions. He would ask a question inquiring if my witness had an opinion about this or that. He would answer yes. Then he would ask, "What is that opinion?" I would then state that we felt compelled to follow the Texas rules on expert opinions; and I instructed the witness not to answer the question. All hell broke loose, and the lawyer threatened both of us with contempt of court and jail. I reminded him that the witness had only been subpoenaed by a notary public, and no court had actually ordered anything. Mad as a wet hen, he built his record with forty-two (Do you have an opinion?) questions. We refused to answer any. He then filed a motion with the California federal judge seeking an order compelling the witness to answer the forty-two questions. He got the order along with one compelling us to reappear on that Friday before the same notary. We did. The FBO lawyer then asked the first of the forty-two questions: i.e., "Do you have an opinion about [whatever]? The witness answered yes. The lawyer then asked, "What is that opinion?" I instructed the witness not to answer. He did not. All hell broke loose for the second time, along with jail threats and the like. I told the lawyer that he had asked one of the forty-two questions requiring a court ordered answer. But the second question asking him to give his opinion was not court ordered, since the lawyer had failed in forty-two instances during the first deposition to ask what the expert's opinion was after having asked if he had an opinion. He made all kinds of threats, but it was nearing five thirty on a Friday afternoon and our El Paso case was scheduled to start at eight o'clock on the following Monday morning. After he had built another record showing the witness refused to answer any of the follow-up questions, we wished him good luck in finding a judge before Monday morning. We told him we would see him in El Paso and he could explain this *hanky panky* California case designed to circumvent the jurisdiction of the Texas court to the judge of the Texas case who he had already found out was a tough old cookie.

On Monday morning, the case proceeded to trial and my first witness was the co-owner of the FBO, who testified at length. My final question to him was whether he had ever turned back the tachometer on this aircraft. He answered absolutely not. I put on numerous witnesses, factual and medical, for the next ten days. All the parties were getting nervous at this point, and each of the three defendants had offered me an expert witness against the others. I would interview them at night; and if they seemed credible, I would use them against whatever defendant their attorney was trying to nail. On the last day of presenting my case for the jury, I recalled the same co-owner of the fixed base operator that I called at the outset of the trial. I told him that I just wanted to be certain of the answer he had given when he first testified. I asked him once again if he had turned back the flight hours shown on the plane's tachometer at any time. He once again consistently said that he absolutely had not. I walked slowly to the back of the court room where the audience sat. One of my associates in the first row handed me a lockbox. I slowly walked back to the witness stand and opened the box. I reached in and slowly removed the visibly charred log book. I thought he was going to have a heart attack, as he instantly knew what it was. I asked him if he recognized it as the internal flight log for the plane in question that he had earlier testified could not be produced since it was lost in fire at their office. He had no choice but to answer yes. I asked him to examine it carefully relative to the hours reflected under the *flight hours* column on two consecutive days. Then I asked him if it were his initials that appeared in the *pilot* column of both of those days. He had no choice but to admit they were his initials. Then I asked him to explain to the jury how

XXX hours at the end of the first day became XX hours at the beginning of the next day. He turned purple and then cold white.

His attorney called for a recess, which the judge granted with the remark that it looked like he really needed one. When he returned, and in front of the jury, he ordered the witness to remove his belongings from the counsel table for lawyers and their clients' representative and sit in audience or go home. He turned to the jury and said that he represented Lloyds of London, the insurance carrier for the FBO and please do not hold the witness against his insurance company. Now the attorney for the airplane manufacturer asked for a recess. He was in the men's room when I went in, and he told me that was the first time in fifty years of trying cases that he had heard a lawyer tell the jury that his true representation was for an insurance company. When we reconvened, I announced that the plaintiffs rested their case. It was the FBO lawyer's turn to put on his defense. His first witness was a metallurgist who was put on out of order since he had been summoned by a congressional committee to testify on his previous prediction that the United States submarine *Thresher* was not seaworthy. It had sunk not long before our trial commenced. He was a qualified witness; however, every time that the lawyer would attempt to focus on a question, the lawyers for the other two defendants would walk up to the evidence table, pick up the charred log book and pass it around among themselves at the counsel table. When the FBO lawyer saw that the jury was following the movement of the log book, rather than listening to his expert, he asked the judge for a further recess to regroup. The judge sensed settlement was close and he granted the recess. Within an hour, I was contacted and told all the defendants had agreed to our current settlement offer and wanted to dictate their agreement into the record. This was done. They then announced to the judge that at the beginning of the trial they had agreed that the case should be settled for our demand amount, but could not agree on their respective proportions of the amount to be paid. After the log book appeared, Lloyds of London stepped up to a much larger share of the settlement and the deal was made.

As a postscript, during the course of discovery and after I had interviewed several of the offered defense experts, I was of the opinion that turning back the tachometer did not have much to do with the crash. The lie turned a weak point into a stronger one, particularly for settlement purposes. Actually what had happened was the engine manufacturer was trying to sell the same front-end version of the engine to Bell to be installed in the interior of a helicopter. Preliminary tests showed that without the front-end air flow, the engine in a helicopter ran hotter and the exhaust valves used in its engine interior installation were sticking frequently. The engine manufacturer reduced the diameter of the exhaust valve, and it solved the helicopter sticking valve problem. However, for reasons best known to the engine manufacturer, it made the smaller diameter exhaust valve standard in its aircraft engines. We later found that the engine manufacturer had reports of fifty-three exhaust valve failures in standard front engine aircraft after reducing the valve diameter. Thus, this was the reason they published the bulletin for owners of such aircraft to replace the smaller exhaust valves with ones with larger diameters that previously had been used. One could have reasonably argued that after fifty-three engine failures due to the breakage of exhaust valves, it should have required that owners of such affected aircraft in operation make the replacement immediately. Of course, chances are that the engine manufacturer would have had to pay for the cost of replacement under such circumstances. Lesson to be learned from this case: For lawyers, *(1) never assume from what a client tells you that there is no adverse documentation anywhere in the woodpile; ask for everything possible that might exist during discovery; (2) when you are trying to build a record for the court to compel an answer from an instructed witness or an otherwise non-*

responsive one, be sure to ask the necessary follow-up questions to reach the ultimate question you want answered; and for lay persons, *never ever fly or ride in a single-engine plane unless you know you can arrive at your intended destination during daylight hours.* Of the other fifty-three single-engine failures reported to the engine manufacturer, there was not a single fatality.

After about eight years of extensive litigation practice, my involvement in banking representation had increased significantly. Thornton Hardie had been the general counsel of El Paso National Bank and a number of neighborhood banks essentially owned by the same shareholders of the downtown bank. When he died, the bank chairman, Sam D. Young, asked me to be the general counsel of their banking interests. This was a major client and Mr. Young nearly always got what he wanted, as he was a dynamic personality and banker. He formed El Paso National Bank in 1925 out of a receivership that he was supervising when he was a national bank examiner for the Comptroller of the Currency. El Paso had 13 banks at that time; and during the depression years all failed except El Paso National Bank and the State National Bank which was the oldest bank in El Paso, having been chartered in 1883.

Mr. Young, who had been born in Woodville, Texas, deep in the piney woods of East Texas, had only an eight-grade education. He had been tremendously successful in banking and business circles. Even from his small base in El Paso, he was a director of Hilton Hotels, El Paso Natural Gas and Texas & Pacific Railway Co., to name a few. He was also a part of a group of Texas and Mexican business persons who purchased the telephone system in Mexico in the early 1960s from Swiss interests. You could walk into any bank in New York City and its top people would know SamYoung, even though some would not know the name of his bank. I traveled with Mr. Young in later years, and to go to the Waldorf Towers or any Hilton Hotel was an experience. He had a solid gold card signed by Conrad Hilton that stated: *Sam Young is my guest at any Hilton Hotel in the world.* Usually, he was recognized immediately at the reception desk as he was a strikingly handsome man with a full head of silver hair. On one occasion he was not recognized by the reception desk; but when he laid his gold card on the table and the clerk called for the assistant manager, about ten persons showed up in about ten seconds to greet him. Sam had banked Conrad Hilton after his hotels had gone bankrupt during the depression. Thornton Hardie was the general attorney for Hilton Hotels until he died. We continued to represent them for many years. Both Sam Young and Thornton Hardie are prominently mentioned in Conrad Hilton's well-known book, *Be My Guest.* Sam Young's incredible career and life has been published by biographer Joseph Leach in *Sun Country Banker: The Life and the Bank of Samuel Doak Young.*

One of the perks flowing from this association with the bank and SamYoung is that we were frequently invited to nightclub with him and Conrad Hilton, and their ladies, when the latter came to El Paso. Conrad loved to dance and he was particularly fond of La Fiesta nightclub in Juarez, Mexico. The club was then in its heyday with many El Paso residents in attendance. It regularly hired big-name performers from the states, and the club management knew how to make its guests feel important. On one occasion at La Fiesta, Sam and Conrad taunted me into singing "Bill Bailey" on stage with the name performer of the evening, Earl Grant. I felt awkward enough, but it got worse about halfway through the song when I spotted one of our firm's senior partners in the audience. He was a no-nonsense lawyer who had formerly been the U. S. attorney in the El Paso area. I had hoped that my singing debut would pass without notice, because I hadn't seen him or anyone else I knew earlier in the evening. Needless to say, everybody at the firm had a good time riding me the next day. I told them to go easy because my performance was a *sacrifice* for two of the firm's best-known clients.

Because banking had become such a large part of my practice, my litigation work had to be held to a minimum.

However, I did handle several important cases during this period. One was to serve as local counsel for a national gypsum company in an antitrust case filed by a local wallboard manufacturer, who was creating shockwaves in the industry by trucking wallboard. Historically, wallboard was priced to move on rail. There were eight defendants in the case, and they were alleged to have violated federal anti-trust laws, the Sherman and Robinson-Patman Acts. The plaintiff had a taped recording of a senior officer of one of the gypsum companies telling the plaintiff's president in a rest room that he represented all the big gypsum companies. He dropped a lot of names of the CEOs of most of the defendants, and then proceeded to tell the plaintiff's president how he should run his business and that trucking was not going to be popular with his gypsum friends. With this tape, the plaintiff could have tried this case before a jury within six months of filing. The major issue then would be whether the other defendants had really authorized the one executive to speak for the group. However, the local firm representing the plaintiff had recently completed a complex case involving Robinson-Patman in another industry, and I suppose they wanted to flex their newly found expertise in this area. The problem, however, is that Robinson-Patman deals with pricing and costing of products; and to make a case, it normally requires years of examining financial records, usually invoices and the like, from all the defendants' business done all in the trade area to ascertain if unjustified price discrimination took place. To make a long story short, this case continued for three years with nearly all the discovery taking place in every party's hot warehouse. Unfortunately for the plaintiff, the lengthy discovery process produced evidence of some well concealed rebates given by it to one of its customers in the building supply business indirectly through its *sister* company with common ownership. The case was settled by each defendant paying a nominal sum, which was less than each defendant's average monthly cost to defend the suit. Sadly, the plaintiff's attorneys had taken this case on a contingency fee arrangement. One-third of a nominal settlement wouldn't have covered their postage and copying costs, much less the efforts of their three excellent attorneys over three years. I was told some years later that the facts of this case were used as background evidence in a criminal trial in Philadelphia filed against the top executives of some of these same defendants.

Another interesting case I tried during this period was in New Mexico. My client was the Lodge in Cloudcroft, New Mexico, a landmark resort situated in the mountains at an altitude of about ten thousand feet. It is truly beautiful and its facilities include a multistory lodge and a nine-hole golf course. The issue involved the ownership of an abandoned railroad right of way that bordered Lodge property and sometimes passed through sections of the golf course. In the early days of El Paso's development there was no air-conditioning. Among the upper class particularly, the husbands sent their families to spend the summer at their cabins in Cloudcroft. The husbands would then take the train to join them for weekends, and then return to work by train from Cloudcroft to El Paso. By the time air-conditioning was plentiful in El Paso, it was no longer necessary to have the family gone for the whole summer. Instead, most families with cabins in Cloudcroft would drive there with their entire families on weekends. Supply and demand change, and thus the demise of the railroad and subsequent abandonment of its right of way occurs.

Two enterprising lawyers, who were also members of the New Mexico legislature, decided that they could make a bundle of money if they could obtain title to the abandoned railroad right of way that so critically affected the Lodge's operations. They obtained a quit-claim deed from the defunct railroad and gave the Lodge notice to move all their operations that were located on the old right of way. Thus, the question that had to be answered was what happens to the ownership of a right of way that has been abandoned by its former owner. The answer depends upon state law, and New Mexico had none on its books. Therefore, this would be a case of first impression in that state. In Texas, we had settled the question long ago due to extensive litigation where the abandoned right of way had oil or gas resources underground below it. The Supreme Court of Texas had held that upon abandonment of any right of way, the ownership in most cases reverted one-half to the landowner on each side of it. If the New Mexico courts would follow the same rule as Texas, the Lodge would have no problem because where the old right of way crossed portions of the golf course (which had been built after the abandonment) it owned the land on both sides, so it would have title to the entire right of way. On the instances where the railroad straddled the borders of the Lodge's property, there would be no problem for the one-half they would be entitled to, since it was the same one-half of the right of way that generally overlapped their property.

The problem was that many states, including Oklahoma, did not follow the Texas solution. Some states say the right of way does not revert to anybody when abandoned; title stays with its owner. That is what the lawyer/lawmakers were counting on. Some states follow a complex rule that recognizes that its owner loses title on abandonment, but it is not split 50/50 and title vests in the owner of one side or the other depending on a number of factors such as which land owner first purchased his adjoining land. This rule would not affect the Lodge on the portions that had been crossed by the right of way, as it owns both sides. However, it would cause them to lose significant portions of land where the right of way ran along its borders.

At that time, the Lodge was owned by Texas residents. I warned my client's owner that we would be somewhat at a disadvantage in the local New Mexico courts since we were not local like the lawmakers. New Mexico has always been known for its politics. Try to get a beer, liquor or law license when you are from out of state. Anyway, the lawmakers filed their suit and it was first heard by the district court in Alamogordo, New Mexico. The case was tried before a judge without a jury. I was rather surprised, but he held in favor of the Lodge and relied on the Texas rule. The case was then appealed to the New Mexico Supreme Court. I applied for permission to present the case before that court for my client. The court granted permission. About the time the case was to be heard before the court, I received a call from my client who told me that he had just learned from reliable sources that our adversaries not only were state legislators, but both were on the committee that determined the budget for the New Mexico Supreme Court. I thanked him for sharing his sinking spell with me. I felt we had been lucky to win at the trial court level; however, it would not have made any difference if we had lost below, since our appeal also would have been to the New Mexico Supreme Court. The day of our appearance before the court arrived and all I could think about was the political aspects of this case. The plaintiffs went first with their oral arguments. As near as I remember they spent nearly as much time referring to the Texas lawyer hired to create bad law for New Mexico as they did arguing the merits of the case. I felt somewhat better when after about the tenth time he commented on the *lawyer from Texas*, the chief justice of the court told him not to waste his limited time by making disparaging remarks about the *distinguished Texas counsel who the court welcomes today*. You could have knocked me over with a feather. To my knowledge, I had never met any member of that court. However, the El Paso Bar, on several occasions, had held joint meetings and dinners with the New Mexico Bar. The bar for El Paso was about the same size as the bar for the State of New Mexico. It then occurred to me that maybe the court just wanted to appear neutral and at the end of the day would rule against us on the merits. When it was my turn to argue, I simply explained the three choices the court had and why I thought the Texas result was the most reasonable way to handle the ownership of abandoned right of ways of any type. Naturally, the court took the decision under advisement. About sixty days later, I received a copy of their decision and they ruled in favor of the Lodge. Lesson to be learned from the case: *even though the cards may look stacked against you, do not be distracted and lose your focus in arguing the law as applied to your facts; justice normally prevails, all things being equal.* I felt guilty about all the thoughts I had harbored throughout this litigation concerning the potential political connection of the legislators to the court system; however, I stayed glued to advocating the sound reasoning behind the Texas courts solution of what is generally called the *Strip-and-Gore* doctrine relating to abandoned right of ways.

Chapter XI

LAW PRACTICE—BUSINESS DEALS

I soon found that one of the most interesting aspects of law practice was the negotiation of business deals, acquisitions and mergers. Making a deal through careful negotiation is an art, not a science. I quickly learned that any lawyer can break a pending deal, but it takes a good one, what I call a *deal lawyer*, to hold a deal together.

First, one must deal with the basics. The result of negotiating is almost universally better when on the buying side of the deal, you are not compelled to buy; and conversely even more so, when on the selling side, you do not have to sell. That creates additional bargaining *power*.

The second principle is that normally one needs to tie a pending deal down tight, so at closing time there are no adverse surprises or wiggle room for the other side to use in order to escape from the deal or to improve it from their standpoint. Having said this, let me add that there are times and circumstances when you have to bend this cookie cutter to meet circumstances. Nearly every problem can be solved someway. In the negotiating process, the display of self-confidence can help set the stage, but it is effective only if you act fairly and in good faith. One also has to develop some tolerance for ambiguity that prevents every piece of a deal from falling in place simultaneously. There may remain a few jagged edges and unresolved minor specifics. Sometimes to be successful in making a worthwhile deal, you must move forward, keeping your eye on the big stuff and knowing that when the major pieces fall together, some minor ambiguity may still exist. Keep the faith, since the major issues are in place and the negotiating game is not necessarily over.

Sometimes, a documented agreement to agree in the future in good faith (even if not immediately binding) can be a more compelling obligation for performance than an unconditional commitment on a point that the other side yielded under pressure. Any ambiguity resulting can work to your advantage, provided you have more tolerance for it than the other side. Every time, however, the other side yields a point under pressure (rather yielding to sound reasoning), their normal reaction will be to try to win multiple future points to justify to themselves and their superiors the loss of the first point. In addition, any point yielded by the other side, through pressure rather than being convinced by logic, may cause them to later make every attempt to avoid the ultimate obligation. Moreover, an agreement that is reached at the negotiating table may not survive further reflection by one side or the other during a recess or an overnight hiatus. Until then, one can only assume the negotiations are moving in the right direction.

If during negotiations, you decide to fold on a negotiating point, do so in a friendly manner. It may soften the other side in ways that are then not apparent. Amazingly, some of the best relationships are often made at the negotiating table as the result of bargaining in good faith. Trust results from one being trustworthy. If you are unable to trust, then look at yourself in the mirror and remember that when you point a finger at someone across the table, there are three of your fingers pointing back at you. Many of our future boosters and sometimes new clients are former adversaries who have been treated firmly, but fairly. There is practically no downside in doing so.

Dollars, on the other hand, that exchange hands at the negotiating table is only money, not necessarily added value. Added value often comes from the relationship established and voluntary future benefits resulting as a by-product of the deal for one side or the other or both. Ultimately, the only good deal for the present and the future as well, is one that both sides have reached at the negotiating table and each thinks it is a good deal for them.

On occasion, you may have to withdraw from the negotiating table to test your bargaining power in a negotiation. One extreme example occurred with a client who was also a good friend. His name was Henry Hicks. He was generous with his family and friends to a point of fault. He owned the Hertz franchises in El Paso and Albuquerque. When he found out I was driving a car with no air-conditioning, he made me promise never to leave town by car without picking up one of his rental units for the trip. We made a number of trips between El Paso and Snyder when air was really needed. The first work I did for Henry was to assist him in negotiating with Hertz, as a member of the franchisees' committee, for a term franchise. In those days, a Hertz franchise was cancelable with thirty days notice from Hertz. We were successful in securing Hertz's agreement to give their franchisees five-year term agreements. This gave the franchise meaningful value to its holder. Not long after that, Hertz found itself in a box when a consent decree limited their horizontal acquisitions from other competitors. Thereafter for the Hertz Corporation to expand, it could only be done by vertically acquiring the business locations of their franchisees.

Henry called me one day and told me that Hertz had asked him to come to New York and talk to them about selling Hertz his two deals. He wanted me to represent him and go with him to the initial meeting in New York. On the way by airplane to New York, I reviewed his financial statements for the last several years. Clearly, his most profitable year was the previous one. I advised him that he should keep it in mind that the Hertz negotiating team, in developing a pricing premium, would first try to average his earnings for several years. This would result in a base earnings amount for a pricing formula that would be substantially less than his past year's earnings standing alone. After further discussion, he told me that he would be willing to sell for the right price, but he did not really care if he did or not. He then laid a heavy burden on me by saying that whatever I felt was the way to go, including selling or not, that's what he wanted to do. I responded that, if it were my deal I would not average the earnings, but would insist on using the past year's results, arguing with Hertz that it was the most current indication of present earning power. Needless to say, it would also be best for my client. Moreover, with the protective shield of a five-year franchise, our bargaining power was now enhanced due to the new five-year-term franchise. In other words, we could negotiate freely without fear of any collateral threat to cancel or not to renew. Lastly, we knew Hertz had no where else to go to buy businesses except from their franchisees. They had already bought out some franchisees in larger cities, including Meyer Brothers on the east coast, which included parking facilities as well as car rental locations. A package of both El Paso and Albuquerque would be more significant to Hertz than most of the other remaining single-city franchises. I told him that if it were my deal I would want ten times the past year's earnings for his deals. He said, "Do what you want; it sounds good to me."

We walked into Hertz's corporate headquarters at 9 AM on a Monday. The conference room was full of Hertz people, including the president and the treasurer. After Henry introduced me to those who I had not previously met during the term franchise negotiations, Hertz led off with the discussion. They mentioned several of their recent acquisitions, including Meyer Brothers. We mentioned the wonderful climate of El Paso and Albuquerque, and the fact that both outlets were located in their respective airport facilities. They told us that as soon as we got business out of the way, we would go to dinner in Connecticut to celebrate a deal at the home of the financial vice president. I suppose that this was an enticement for a quick surrender. They then brought in another player, who was a retired Hertz executive who Henry had known for a long time. He was their chief negotiator. After reviewing Henry's financials for an hour or so, the negotiator said that a fair deal, in his opinion, would be a sum two times the last three years average earnings. I took Henry to the side and we talked strategy. We went back to the table and I told them that in my opinion, a fair pricing formula for both cities would be a sum equal to ten times the previous year's earnings. Their reaction seemed to imply that they were of the opinion that a country lawyer had just come to New York City on the back of a turnip truck. The negotiator told us that they only had to pay two and one-half times average earnings for three years for Meyer Brothers, and that included parking garages. They didn't see how they could now pay Henry a higher multiple. Maybe so, we responded, but the deal we were taking about was not Meyer Brothers. I suggested that if they had made the favorable purchase they indicated, they should factor that bargain into this deal, and in that way average their cost for Meyer Brothers and both of Henry's two deals. By averaging their bargain deal with the proposed two-city deal they deemed less favorable, it might massage their mental processes to view the price paid for their last three deals as reasonable. At this point, we excused ourselves to let them ponder our position, and we went back to the hotel.

Every day that week at 9 AM we went to Hertz's offices. We replayed the game over and over; and near midweek all their negotiating team could predict that we would walk no later than 10:30 AM. We had more fun than imaginable for the rest of every day. I had never been to New York, and Henry had been there many times over the years. We would take a nap. Then we would go to Jack Dempsey's restaurant for an early drink and oysters. We would then go to a Broadway show. After the show, we went to a fine restaurant for a late dinner. Finally, about 2 AM we would walk across the street from the Plaza Hotel where we were staying to Central Park. Before we would leave each night we ordered raw carrots by the dozen from room service. They thought we were crazy Texans. We carried the carrots to Central Park and fed them to our favorite carriage horse, which was showing years of wear of pounding his heavy hoofs on the paved streets of Central Park. After feeding this horse (we called him "Mr. Ed") each evening, we would retire about 2:30 AM in order to resume our 9 AM ritual with Hertz. We left the following Sunday with no deal or other result but two well-fed guys from El Paso and one well-fed old horse in Central Park.

Not by coincidence, I am sure, but the first week back in El Paso I developed a bleeding ulcer. When I got to the hospital, they said I had lost one-half of my blood by volume and they were dangerously close to having to give me a transfusion. My doctor, who was also my next door neighbor, told the nurses to check me regularly through the night, and, if they thought I needed a transfusion, to call him at home. I can remember awaking and seeing the nurses bending over me. Fortunately, I recovered sufficiently that I did not need the transfusion.

On the Friday I was due to be discharged from the hospital, the full negotiating team for Hertz came to El Paso. In my hospital room, we made the deal, ten times the previous year's earnings, which was precisely the deal we had first offered to Hertz in New York City. Henry also wanted Hertz stock and not cash. He got a bundle. Shortly thereafter the deal was enhanced even further when RCA acquired Hertz. Henry then held a bundle of RCA stock, which reflected another premium on the Hertz stock acquired by RCA. This was certainly a unique negotiation, but one heck of a lot of fun as well as profitable.

Henry told me to send him a bill and be generous with myself on the fee. I thought about it and send him an invoice for $25,000. When Henry received it, he called me and said he would not pay it. I told him any invoice I sent a client only represented what I felt the work was worth considering the time expended and, on occasion, the result obtained. It was not owed unless the client was also satisfied. I asked him how much of a reduction to the invoice would make him a happy camper. He told me the only invoice he would pay was twice that amount, $50,000. I reluctantly obliged him and I never had that happen again in my years of practice. I will never forget Henry Hicks, as he was a true friend and mentor due to our age difference. I also never will forget that he died on September 7, 1970.

September 7 by coincidence is the birthday of another client that I acquired by a series of circumstances, and this client would change my life forever. One of the lawyers in our firm represented his father, Fred Schneider Jr., who had come to El Paso to buy the Pontiac dealership about the same time that I moved to El Paso to practice law. I knew his son, Fred D. Schneider, from playing golf at Coronado Country Club where we were members. Over the years we had become friends. About 1962, the father died playing golf about a block from his house and about one-half block from his doctor's house. I assisted the dad's attorney in our firm with the federal estate tax return and subsequent audit. We got a good audit result largely based on the fact that an automobile franchise at that time was typically terminated by the manufacturer upon death of the *dealer operator* named in it. This had occurred in our case prior to the filing and subsequent IRS audit of the estate tax return. It was a *new* franchise that the manufacturer executed with his son.

One of the first things, Fred did was to buy a small Piper Navajo airplane, which he flew himself. He took my partner, who had represented his father and the dealership, on several short business trips. My partner had a mild heart condition and normally would not fly at all. One day he came into my office and asked if I would be willing to take over the Schneider's representation. I told him it was fine with me if it was alright with Fred. It was.

I represented him in a number of various business deals over the years. In an early one, he and another El Paso automobile dealer had contacted a broker in Dallas to purchase a limited capital life insurance company from the state's former governor and U.S. senator, W. Lee O'Daniel. I told Fred that I remembered O'Daniel from the early days in Snyder when he would come to the town's square to politic for some race. He traveled with a western band known as the *Light Crust Doughboys*. The whole town turned out for the show, all three thousand of them. He always won his political race, but nobody would admit that they voted for him. After we worked out the terms of the contract with the broker and it had been signed by all parties, we prepared for the closing which was to take place on a specified future date in the office of the executive vice president of Mercantile National Bank in Dallas. When the date came, we flew in Fred's airplane (which by then had been updated to a Cessna 421) to Dallas and made our way to the bank's office building. The executive vice president was cordial, but said that he had not heard from Senator O'Daniel recently. The broker showed up and he was surprised that the senator was not there. He called his house and talked at length with him. It appeared that the senator had forgotten the closing date, but he did want us to come to his house to do the deal as he needed the money for his son's (Pat) current race for governor of Texas. We all made our way to the senator's home, which was actually an apartment in a complex he owned. We knocked on the door, and it was belatedly answered by the senator's wife. She knew we were coming and invited us in. It was pitch dark in the apartment except for a faint light coming from a Tiffany lamp in one corner. I later checked it and the lamp had a 25-watt bulb in it. Everything was weird, and it was all we could do to keep from laughing in front of Mrs. O'Daniel.

We sat around the dark room for nearly thirty minutes waiting for the senator to appear. Finally, he entered the room carrying a ledger record book purporting to contain the financial information needed for us to examine in order to close the purchase of the limited capital life insurance company. He handed it over for our inspection. Fred and I both looked at it. We are both graduate accountants and it didn't take us long to see that the last entry posted was two years before. We explained to the broker that the books had not been posted for two years; and that had to be done. We also needed the company's tax returns filed for the company for the past three taxable years. At this point, the senator stated that he had been waiting for the man who did the posting to bring it up to date, but that guy was still sweeping out portions of the apartment complex. If the price had not been right, I am sure we would have packed up and left for El Paso at that point. We asked how long it would take for the janitor to post the transactions in the books and to prepare the required financial statements. The senator didn't know when his janitor would have enough time to do all of this, but he said that he could show us how to close the books. At this point, he took a large metal clip from his desk drawer and put it over the front and back covers of the ledger book, saying, "Now the books are closed!"

With that display of accounting expertise, we told the broker to get busy and get the deal ready for closing on a future date; and we would only come back when he could personally assure us the deal was ready to close. We then flew back to El Paso, but we were on the floor of the plane laughing our fool heads off. The pilot had a metal clip holding some flight materials together, and we temporarily borrowed it to reenact the senator's closing of his company books. If one were not present at our abbreviated meeting with the senator, they would never believe what happened. Eventually, we did close the deal after our CPA had inspected the records, posted the old transactions himself and decided there was no substantial risk in closing. It turned out that the only activity the company had was to carry life insurance on the lives of a few orphans. The senator then personally paid all the premiums to keep the company qualified as a life insurance company under the Texas Insurance Laws. The company was appropriately named the *Texas Star Life Insurance Company*.

The next deal I handled for Fred was the purchase of the local Cadillac dealership which was still located near downtown El Paso, and General Motors wanted it moved to Montana Street in the eastern part of the city. Its owner was Mitch McClure, a large chain GM dealer who had over the years owned sixty-nine GM stores all over the country. Mitch wanted to sell the dealership facility which he owned personally and the dealership assets which were owned by his corporation. After a price was agreed upon for both items, I worked the contract details out with Mitch's local lawyer whose brother was to be the closer for the title company on the real estate. When we inspected the deal, we found a few discrepancies in the *other assets* of the financials, but Mitch told us not to worry about them, pay his price or forget the deal. He went on to tell us of the many deals he had bought and sold, and he said that he had learned a valuable lesson in making deals: *remember there is always a little good and a little bad in every deal.* We had apparently discovered the *little bad.* There was not enough money at issue to let the deal get away, so we proceeded with the closing after Mitch used his influence to get GM to approve the sale. Factories often drag their corporate feet because there is always some factory patsy in line to buy good deals that come up for sale. Mitch went to the home of a GM executive to get the sale approved. He succeeded in doing so.

When we got to the title company, Mitch, his lawyer and the lawyer's brother, who was the closer, were there. We examined the closing papers for the sale of the corporation and the real estate. After looking them over, I whispered to Fred that I had found a *little good* in the deal. The corporation had leased the real estate from Mitch under a triple net lease, which meant that among other things the dealership had to pay property taxes. They were rather substantial because it was close to downtown. The property taxes had been accrued on the dealership's financials, which meant its book value (and our purchase price for the dealership) had been reduced under the purchase formula by the amount of that expense accrual. However, the closer at the title company had prorated the same taxes again in the real estate transaction, which meant the amount of the accrued taxes had been deducted as an offset to the real estate purchase price. The result was that in the overall transaction, we had received credit for the same amount of property taxes twice. The deal closed smoothly and everyone parted cordially.

We went to lunch afterwards with Harold Bailey, a banker who was resigning his job to become Fred's partner in the Cadillac dealership. I told Harold what had happened and suggested he cut a check for the amount of the excessive tax credit we had received and just hold it. Having been around Mitch for several weeks, I predicted that within a short period of time Harold would get a call from him telling Harold that he had been double dipped in the transaction for accrued and prorated taxes. We told Harold that what Fred and I wanted him to do was to tell Mitch after expressing surprise: *Well Mitch, now I know what you meant when you told us that there is always a little good and a little bad in a deal. And you were right, we found some of both.* After Mitch blew sky high, we told Harold to send him the check so he could see it was all in good humor and that we never intended to keep the unintended tax benefit. In less than two weeks, the call from Mitch came just as predicted. Harold played out our little joke very seriously, and Mitch blew up as predicted. When he got the predated check the next day by overnight mail, not only was Mitch relieved but we had made a very good friend.

Another interesting association in El Paso came as a result of my representation of Azar Nut Company, which was then the third largest nut processor in the nation and was owned by twin brothers, Ed and Phil Azar. Initally, Ed had asked me to represent the company in negotiating its sale to

Consolidated Food Co., which was in an acquisition mode at the time. In fact, our negotiations were with a *vice president in charge of acquisitions* of Consolidated. The deal was negotiated and closed in the due course of time. The Azar brothers received a large block of Consolidated securities and were obligated to stay on for a period of time in order to prepare successors for their positions. In the meantime, the more familiar Consolidated became with the complexities of the nut-processing business, the more concerned it became with the prospects of long-term success in the business without the Azars. The nut-processing business is not as simple as packing nuts and selling the product through retail outlets and to airplane carriers in attractive packages for their passengers. Not only is the business highly competitive, but there are other perils such as acquiring the nuts to be processed in the first place. At that time, Azar contracted with nut growers in various parts of the world. Any nut processor has probably experienced some of the perils in sourcing from other countries. For example, a nut processor contracts in India for a future delivery of a specified quantity of pistachio nuts at a negotiated price. The time of delivery arrives but the then current value in the market for pistachios is much higher than the agreed-upon purchase price. It was not uncommon for the foreign grower to demand more money prior to scheduled delivery. How would you like to go to India to enforce a valid contract? Therefore, practically you usually paid a price between the contract and current market price to the foreign grower, because it is late in the processing cycle; and if you bought elsewhere this late in the season, you would pay market value anyway. Conversely, if the price dropped before shipment, you have two chances to get a price concession from the foreign grower—slim and none. In addition, there is a lot of expertise, savvy and personal attention to develop a loyal group of domestic growers. These were probably some of the problems that began to trouble Consolidated about their long term future in the nut-processing business.

In any event, Consolidated again approached the Azars—this time about repurchasing the business. This suited the twins just fine, as working for someone is never the same as ownership. Once again, the brothers asked me to represent them in the repurchase. We got even a better deal this time. First, the price was right. Secondly, Consolidated agreed to take Azars' note, secured by the same Consolidated shares it had issued to the brothers when it orginally bought the company. Thirdly, we negotiated a provision that the Azars had the option at any time to use the stock, at its market value, to pay off the note. Finally, we negotiated a provision that regardless of market value at the time of any partial or full note payoff using the stock, each share had a specified *minimum* value for that purpose. Thus the Azars had the comfort level of knowing that they could pay off the note at any time for no less than the stock's stated minimum value.

When the repurchase was complete, the Azar brothers approached me about an idea they had after it became apparent that they were going to be co-owners of the business again. Like all siblings, the twins did not always see eye to eye, particularly on some business decisions. Consequently, even though the company was 100 percent owned by them, they had agreed that it would be a good idea to have a board of directors that essentially would have a majority of outside directors. They asked the recently retired executive vice president of Safeway food stores, the then current president of the Lucky Boy food chain from California and me to serve as outside directors. We all agreed to do so. I learned a lot about the nut business serving on this board and the spirit of cooperation was outstanding. I have never seen a private company with the majority of the directors being nonowners, but if the results could always be as good as this effort, I would highly recommend it. Differences between the brothers Azar seemed to become extinct. I had the pleasure of serving on this board for a number of years and until I left El Paso to move to Houston.

Chapter XII

TRANS TEXAS BANCORPORATION

In the early 1970s, the Texas Banking Commission finally abandoned its previous position that multibank holding companies violated the branch banking prohibition of the Texas banking laws. There was a rush throughout the state, and about the same time throughout all of the southern states that also prohibited branch banking, to form multibank holding companies. From the inception of Texas as a state, the rural bankers had enough political clout in the state legislature to keep branch banking out of the state, as they didn't want their respective little banking kingdoms to be gobbled up by the big city banks. Sam Young almost immediately called me after the Texas Banking Commission changed its position to a meeting in his office with him, his son and his principal shareholders to discuss the establishment of a bank holding company.

Sam and his business associates, who had controlled El Paso National Bank since they organized it in 1925, had together owned more than 50 percent of the stock of three neighborhood banks—First State Bank, Northgate National Bank and Border City Bank—throughout the years since the organization of each. Two family groups, the Youngs and the Harveys, owned almost 30 percent of the stock of El Paso National Bank and the Youngs alone controlled over 25 percent of the shares of the three neighborhood banks. Many of the employees of the three neighborhood banks were former employees of El Paso National Bank, and two of the top officers of Northgate National Bank were related to Sam. When only two of the thirteen banks in El Paso survived the Great Depression, El Paso National Bank had an approximate 25 percent share of the total El Paso banking market and State National Bank, founded forty-two years earlier than Sam's bank, had the remaining 75 percent of that market. But when we first met in Sam's office in 1971 with him and his colleagues to discuss the formation of a multi-bank holding company, Sam's four controlled banks had become the largest factor in the El Paso market with over a 41 percent share of the total market: all of the then thirteen other banks in town shared the balance of it.

As a result of this 1971 initial meeting, it was decided to pursue as soon as possible the formation of a multi-bank holding company. It was to be named Trans Texas Bancorporation, Inc. The initial board of directors and officers were the two Youngs and me. We then applied to the Federal Reserve Board for approval of its becoming a bank holding company through the acquisition of El Paso National Bank and the three neighborhood banks. Although the Department of Justice opposed our application on grounds the combined organization would control over 41 percent of the El Paso banking market, the board held that the four banks were under such a degree of common ownership that there was no significant existing competition between them. The Federal Reserve Board then, on February 29, 1972, approved our application as in the public interest.

Our progress to form and implement our bank holding company was short lived, because on March 29, 1972, the Antitrust Division of the Department of Justice filed suit in the federal district court for the Western District of Texas in El Paso, staying the consummation of the proposed transaction. The suit, *United States of America v. Trans Texas Bancorporation, Inc., El Paso National Bank, First State Bank, Northgate National Bank of El Paso and Border City Bank*, alleged that the proposed acquisition by Trans Texas of the four banks would have a significant adverse effect on competition in the El Paso banking market in violation of Section 7 of the *Clayton Act*, 15 U.S. Code 18. The government also alleged that if the four banks remained separate the common ownership that existed would not likely be permanent in view of the advanced age of Sam Young; however, if the banks were united under the umbrella of the holding company, that consolidation would be permanent. The latter was exactly the reason we wanted to form Trans Texas, and it would also allow Trans Texas to acquire future banks elsewhere with less problems than having to first assemble a group of shareholders to do so.

Sam asked what I though our chances were to prevail. I told him that I thought we could prove the reality of our common ownership, and that we were fortunate not to be sued for any violation of Section 1 of the *Sherman Act*, 15 U.S. Code 1, for price fixing practices among the four banks. The 1 Sherman combined with 7 Clayton allegations had slowed down a case filed before the Trans Texas suit by the government against Citizens & Southern National Bank in Atlantic, Georgia. I further advised Sam that in at least one 1 Sherman case, *United States v. Yellow Cab Co.*,332 U.S. 218, the Supreme Court had held that common ownership of two or more price fixing entities was not a defense to a 1 Sherman violation. In other words, a business entity must find new customers by competing successfully rather than arranging treaties with its competitors through corporate interrelationships. As far as 7 Clayton was concerned, there was not a single case on the books that dealt with the common ownership issue, and therefore we would be dealing with an issue of first impression unless the C&S case was decided before our case went to trial. If not, we would be dealing with logic and facts in formulating our defense for the proposed consolidation as we walked through the legal minefield where the courts had not previously ventured.

We would want to advance significant common sense reasons why the Trans Texas acquisition would not "lessen competition" such as the fact that the common ownership of our banks had been continually in existence since each bank was formed; therefore, no real competition had developed among them or would likely be developed in the future. But with no legal precedent to guide us in this case, it would be a real crap shoot to predict how the case would be ultimately decided. I shook Sam up somewhat when I told him the government had not lost a single 7 Clayton case in over twenty-two years, and this fact alone would give the Antitrust Division of the Department of Justice a lot of comfort in vigorously prosecuting our case. Sam said he was counting on me to change that statistic, and that he wanted to proceed with the trial as soon as possible.

From that point on, we were buried in the discovery phase of the trial. Due to Sam's marching orders, I filed a motion with the federal judge, Ernest Guinn, who was known as an extremely pro-government judge, to set the trial at the earliest possible date and we would be ready to proceed. At this hearing on an expedited trial setting, the government filled the courtroom with numerous posters on the walls and on easels which reflected for every bank merger or acquisition case in history the date it was filed by the government and the date that trial commenced. The average of the hundred cases was something like two and one-half years from the date of filing to trial. I asked Judge Guinn for trial in six months or less. Judge Guinn set the trial date for September 25,1972, four days shy of the normal six months minimum called for at the time in the Manual of Complex Litigation. The government lawyers vigorously protested, but Judge Guinn told them that none of the hundred of cases that had been cited was tried in his court; and that the way he kept his docket clean was to try cases as soon as possible, particularly with all the drug and immigration cases that naturally occur in and around the international border separating El Paso from Mexico. He also reminded them that it was the government who filed the suit, and its attorneys must have had some idea what it was that the defendants did or didn't do when it was filed.

The government responded to the granting of our motion to expedite trial by marshalling their vast resources to work on the case, hoping to pressure us to ask for a delay due to the intense discovery barrage they then leveled at us. Our firm had then about twenty-two lawyers, and everybody had more work than they could say grace over. We were horribly outnumbered, but there was no way we were going to give up our trial setting. I would rather work 24-7 (which just about was the case) than tell Sam Young that I was going to request a delay. Either option could be unpleasant. Instead, I asked my partner, John Grambling to sit through the eventual trial with me, since he had more experience in federal court than I and two heads in the heat of battle are better than one. I then assembled the brightest young men and women working for the banks to form a paralegal team to assist in handling the mountains of documents required to meet numerous deadlines. We formed a second group of bankers to go back through the stock transfer records of all four of the banks and put together a computerized record of stock ownership for each bank since its inception. Some of these very competent bank personnel handled their bank duties during the day and worked long hard hours for me at night during the six months before the scheduled trial date.

When the trial date arrived, the government attorneys were still filing discovery requests in an attempt to prevent the case from going to trial. Most of their requests were meaningless but required numerous man-hours to comply. Judge Guinn would not cut us any slack, so we continued to maintain our paralegal task force now working to retrieve data during the day while we were in trial. We would join them at night to analyze the data and prepare response documents. This group did not miss a single deadline before or during the trial. The trial took ten days. The government relied mainly on the absence of any legal precedence and the testimony of a Michigan law professor who was also an economist. I used the president of the competing State National Bank Group (who wanted to do the same type of consolidation down the road) to testify that his bank didn't have any objection or see any elimination of competition in the formation of Trans Texas. I supported his testimony with that of Tom Frost, a banker from San Antonio, Texas, who testified that he felt that bank holding companies would be very beneficial for Texas banking since we were not allowed to branch bank. As an expert witness, I used a University of Tennessee law professor who was also an economist to offset the government's Michigan professor. Neither of them would admit to the time of day to counsel opposing them. We closed by introducing a complete record of the four banks' stock ownership from the inception of each. A granddaughter of Mr. Young, who was working at the bank during summer vacation from college, had been in charge of the paralegal group working on this project.

We had no idea how long it would take Judge Guinn to decide the case. He had never had to write a full-written opinion as it is seldom needed at the district court level and the entry of an order usually suffices. After deciding the case, we had no idea how long it would take him to write his first opinion. Frankly, we got the answer sooner than I expected. Judge Guinn ruled in our favor in a written opinion filed on November 13, 1972. Thus, in less than eight months from the date the government filed its suit, we had a verdict.

The government filed a direct appeal to the United States Supreme Court asking it to set aside the lower court's verdict and to render verdict for the United States of America. Just to be involved in any case in the Supreme Court is awesome and somewhat breathtaking. There were things to do that I had never had to do before. First, I made a trip to Washington, DC to request the United States attorney general to drop the appeal as Trans Texas was small fish compared to the major banks in Texas and C&S in Atlanta, whose case was still dragging far behind us. I could hardly field the telephone calls from banks and their attorneys. However, none of them offered to help foot the expense of the appeal. But they all wanted to be kept informed of our progress. As anticipated the attorney general gave thumbs down to our request for them to withdraw their notice of appeal. My next trip was also to Washington, DC to visit with Dean Griswold, the solicitor general of the United States whose staff would be directly in charge of the case for the government before the Supreme Court. Dean Griswold formerly had been the dean of the Harvard Law School. He was very warm and cordial, but he told me he was a lame duck as solicitor general as Robert Bork was soon to replace him. Consequently, he pointed in the direction of about seven staffers sitting around room and told me it would be their decision whether to pursue the appeal. One look at that crowd did not say anything for my chances to gain a favorable decision from them.

Dean Griswold dismissed them after hearing my pitch and then invited me into his private office. He showed me pictures of his grandchildren and a lot of memorabilia. We then sat down to visit and he told me that he personally felt that I had a point that there were bigger fish to fry than Trans Texas. He also acknowledged that if the decision was his personally to make, he might not risk taking our relatively small case before the Supreme Court in a case of first impression. He was the first person in the government that had ever acknowledged to me that it was at least possible that they might lose their first 7 Clayton case since 1950 to a small-town player. If so, the results could be very bad, as the doors for this type of bank consolidation would be wide open for all the really big guys to walk through. He also said that he preferred branch banking to bank holding companies. I agreed, but told him the rural bankers in Texas had prevented that through out time. I told him that branching would be far less expensive than consolidation with the formation of bank holding companies. Both forms of consolidation require a physical facility, but with a bank holding company each subsidiary must maintain its separate capital. A bank branch requires a physical plant only. Having agreed on about everything except the reason I came to Washington in the first place, we shook hands and parted. Each of us knew what the staffers' decision on appeal would be. And that was the way it came down.

It was now time to begin preparing our brief to the Supreme Court. I asked Sam Young for permission to engage a firm with a lot of Supreme Court experience to hold my hand and review my brief, as well as to provide the necessary nomination for my admission to the bar of the United States Supreme Court. He agreed; and in fact, he had a friend with the prestigious New York law firm of Sullivan & Cromwell, who he felt would stand by for those duties at a fairly nominal fee. Sam Young never lived long enough to enjoy paying legal fees. On June 25, 1973, I received my certificate of admission to the Supreme Court bar upon the nomination of Roy H. Steyer of Sullivan & Cromwell. This almost came after the fact, since I had already briefed the case, had it reviewed by Sullivan & Cromwell and had filed it with the Supreme Court. On the last day of its term that summer, the Court surprised us with a six-to-three decision in favor of Trans Texas. The government had lost its first 7 Clayton case since 1950. Immediately, bankers and antitrust lawyers from all over the country, shocked by this unexpected reversal of antitrust litigation, besieged Sam and me with questions about how on earth we accomplished this result. I remember one such call from the attorneys representing General Dynamics Corp. in a nonbank case, and they felt the barn door had been knocked down against significant mergers in general due to our six-to-three decision. It was also the first bank merger case in which Justice William Powell had voted. Previously, he had abstained from voting due to previous representation of a Virginia bank when he was in private practice in Richmond, Virginia.

Things did change dramatically from the restrictive days of mergers being bad just because they were big. During the next term, the Supreme Court approved the General Dynamics case in *United States of America v. General Dynamics Corp.*, 415 U.S. 605 (1974). Finally, on June 17, 1975, the Supreme Court ruled in favor of C&S in its bank holding company case, which involved not only 7 Clayton but also1 Sherman. In that decision, the Supreme Court cited the *Trans Texas* case as authority under the 7 Clayton portion and also held for the bank on the 1 Sherman count in *United States of America v. Citizens & Southern National Bank*, 422 U.S. 86 (1975).

Since that time I cannot count the ever growing number of big and important mergers that have been permitted. I cannot help but recall Dean Griswold's concern about the risk from trying the little guys first. I also remembered that he told me his only concern about our transaction was that if we were successful, it would not be long until some larger banking organization acquired the Trans Texas group. I told him that would never happen, as we would be busy acquiring other banks. Guess what? He was right. After forming several more subsidiaries and after the holding company's Trans Texas name was changed to the El Paso National Corp., it was acquired by Texas Commerce Bancshares, Inc. in Houston. Texas Commerce Bank was then acquired by Chemical Bank of New York. Chemical Bank was merged with Chase National Bank of New York, which has now merged with JPMorgan Bank of New York, resulting in JPMorgan Chase Bank. That organization has now merged with Banc One. These consolidations far exceed the worst fears of Dean Griswold in 1973; I would enjoy crossing paths with one or more of his staffers who felt there was no risk in appealing the *Trans Texas* case. I doubt if I could keep from saying to them, "I tried to tell you so!"

Chapter XIII

AUTOMOBILE DEALER

By the time we had completed the Trans Texas litigation, I had a number of things that were running through my mind. First, my law practice had developed to such a point with extraordinary clients that it was increasing difficult to allocate my time among them to the extent they desired. I also had the sense that I had accomplished everything in the practice of law that I had originally hoped to do, and I was somewhat concerned that my future in law might not be as fulfilling as the past sixteen years or so. In addition, with the advent of computers becoming increasingly common around a law firm and with the increased emphasis on fee generation in the legal profession in general, I felt that gradually the law profession was drifting more and more to becoming a business. Due to the growth of our firm in recent years, my interviewing and training responsibilities to the firm and the talented young men we had hired were only compounding my personal time problem. I could refer more and more to these young men to help allocate my time to practice personally; however, this did not do much for my personal income from the firm. Finally, I had invested in a Toyota dealership with Fred Schneider, and I felt some resentment building in a few of the numerous other automobile dealers I personally represented. To make a long story longer, Fred and I had talked several times about me becoming involved in the actual management of a dealership. This would require we find one large enough for both of us and would not displace other key people he had developed over the years, such as Harold Bailey at the Cadillac dealership and J. T. Gilbert, his long-time friend and associate who had first worked for Fred's father when he was sixteen years old.

Fred and I made a number of trips to California looking for a large dealership. However, the ones we found available did not appeal to us due to either location or franchise brand. We also knew that import market penetration was sky rocketing on the West Coast, and felt it would be difficult to make it with domestic franchises only. Nobody wanted to part with a good import franchise that was well located. If they were willing to sell, they wanted more money than the deal appeared to be worth.

So I continued to practice law for the next several years, and was elected president-elect of the El Paso Bar Association in 1976. Ironically, I would never serve as president, since in the fall of 1976 the kind of deal Fred and I were looking for appeared almost like magic. Lester Goodson, a prominent Houston dealer who owned the fourth largest sales volume Pontiac store in the nation, was also a pioneer in developing quarter horse racing. The biggest event of the year for those racing fans and horses was the All-American Futurity held on Labor Day each year in Ruidoso, New Mexico. In 1976, Lester borrowed a car from Fred to drive from the El Paso airport to Ruidoso for the Futurity. On the way to Ruidoso, which is about a two-and-one-half hour drive from El Paso, Lester wrecked the car. He called Fred and asked him to call his partner, Ruskin Smith, in Houston and work out the insurance details concerning the accident. In talking with Ruskin, Fred asked, as he nearly always did in talking with large city dealers, if Ruskin knew of any good deals for sale in Houston. Ruskin replied that it was some coincidence that he would ask, as the last thing he and Lester had discussed before the trip was selling their dealership. Earlier, the plan for succession was that Ruskin would buy Lester's share of the deal someday and have his son-in-law named as the dealer-operator of the deal. Ruskin and his wife, Doris, had three daughters. But that plan had then recently been abandoned when the son-in-law had become a paraplegic while body surfing in Hawaii.

As soon as Lester was back in Houston, Fred and I flew there to meet with him and Ruskin. Lester met us at the airport and handed Fred a small sheet of paper that looked like a page from a desk calendar that outlined what he wanted for his deal. Lester was a man of few words and he didn't have much tolerance for details. The sheet contained the estimated market price for his eleven and one-half acres of land on which the dealership was located, plus he wanted to sell his corporation for its book value, excluding the book value of the land for which he wanted market value. There was no asking price for blue sky. This deal was too good to be true. We went to his office, and he told us that he knew that he could get quite a bit of blue-sky premium for the deal, but he didn't need it nor did Ruskin. What they both wanted was *cash on the barrel head.* He said a lot of people, including the local Pontiac zone manager, had tried to buy his deal over the years, but their propositions were either too complicated for Lester to bother with or they required him to finance a portion of the sales price. He wanted to handpick his buyer and wanted the buyer to have a good deal. Lester was one in a million.

I saw a massive will on his desk, which he said had been drafted by his attorneys, Vinson & Elkins, a large Houston firm, but he wasn't going to sign it because it was too long and complicated. He lived in Conroe, Texas and also had a ranch in Magnolia, Texas. He said he knew a country lawyer in Conroe, and he would ask him to prepare a simple will leaving everything to his wife. He only had one daughter, and she and her husband were financially independent. I tried to encourage him to call his regular firm and tell them what he wanted and listen to the potential pitfalls in his desire for a simple will. He didn't say no, but I could see he had no intention of doing that. We ate lunch, shook hands on the deal and told Lester and Ruskin we would be back the next day with a contract. On the way back to El Paso that afternoon, I told Fred that although we were buying his corporation, we would had to have an abbreviated contract, which would involve some risk to us; or we would end up like Vinson & Elkins. I knew that it would be the toughest contract I had ever drafted, because it would need some strong representations and warranties by Lester to protect us against contingencies, claims, taxes and undisclosed liabilities and/or nonexistent assets. Yet, I had already made up my mind that the agreement would not exceed two pages. Fred agreed and we both felt that Lester and Ruskin were extremely honorable men and the deal was too fantastic to pass. However, it still involved several million of dollars that we did not have. Sam Young was in La Jolla, California, at his summer residence. We called him immediately, and he said he would either bank it or have Ben Love, CEO of Texas Commerce Bank in Houston bank it since Houston real estate was involved. But one way or the other, Sam told us to write the check for whatever and whenever we needed it; and he would make the financing happen.

I stayed up half the night or better drafting and rewriting the contract. I finally had it reduced to one and one-half pages, and still felt that on the really important parts, I had strong and significant representations and warranties, albeit briefly stated. We went back the next day to Houston and signed the deal on Fred's birthday, September 7. While in Houston that day, we went with Lester to the Pontiac zone office and presented the contract to the zone manager to commence the approval process. Since he had hoped to buy the deal somehow, someway and someday, he was not a happy camper; but after extended discussions with Lester and with us, he said he would notify Pontiac in Detroit at his leisure. In the meantime, we checked with friends in Houston and found that Lester's estimated market value of the land was probably less than actual market value. It now appeared that at the time we closed the deal, we could buy the land and the buildings (the latter priced at depreciated book value which clearly was an understated value) from Lester's corporation and then mortgage the real estate for enough to pay the entire cash purchase price for the land and corporation from the mortgage proceeds.

We did just that and closed the deal on October 20, 1976. Most of the delay was due to delaying tactics by General Motors in giving its approval, but they finally realized that Lester was going to stand fast with us as his chosen buyers. They also knew by past experience dealing with us that if necessary, we would file an action with the Texas Motor Vehicle Commission in Austin to accelerate their decision-making process. Out of the first eight cases filed with the Commission after the enabling legislation protecting franchised motor vehicle dealers from arbitrary acts of the franchisor was passed in 1965, I filed five of those cases for various automobile dealers in El Paso. All five cases had a successful result for my clients. GM correctly assumed that due to my personal involvement in this one, justice would be both likely and swift.

The hardest part of my decision to switch careers from law to business was the task of telling my law partners. I started with John Grambling and Bill Mounce, as we had become best of friends as well as partners over the years. The three of us also were the firm's executive committee. They didn't like what I had to say, but understood that my mind was made up and they wished me well. I made my way through the rest of the firm, and the most difficult part was informing the young men I had recruited for the firm during the past years that I was abandoning ship. Finally, the task was done, but we agreed that I would keep my practice open until the end of the year and officially resign from the partnership as of January 1, 1977. This also gave me some time to wrap up some loose ends on cases and transactions I was handling and to work with my partners and clients on attorney assignments for any unfinished business. Of course, Sam Young knew about the change and had already been raising hell with Fred for *stealing* his general counsel. I sat down with Sam and my partner, Bill Mounce, who was a very solid lawyer and had done bank work from time to time. Sam agreed that Bill would be man to replace me as general counsel and this was important to me. I assured Sam that the transition would be smooth and I would remain as a director and officer of Trans Texas and attend its monthly meetings as long as he needed me. I did so, until the banks were sold in 1983 to Texas Commerce Bank. In addition, I was elected to the board of directors of Texas Commerce Bank—North Freeway when I moved to Houston. It was a neighborhood bank which was owned by Texas Commerce Bancshares, a bank holding company that owed its existence to the fact that the Department of Justice's teeth had been pulled by the Supreme Court's decision in the *Trans Texas* case.

In the course of time, Fred and I worked twelve-hour days during 1977 and made all the changes we felt necessary to the operations of Lester Goodson Pontiac. We had been there about six months when a zone manager from American Honda paid us a visit. We knew that Lester Goodson Pontiac also had a Honda franchise, but in those days that was no big deal. We did not even bother to secure Honda's approval to the change in corporate ownership before we closed the purchase from Lester. That could have been grounds for cancellation of our Honda franchise. However, since the franchise was operated by the Pontiac dealership as a dual product we had continued to receive and sell a few Hondas from the Goodson used car lot facility. The Honda zone manager looked around and told us it looked like there had been a few changes; and didn't we think it would be a good idea to bring the paper work up to date? We thought that would be alright if it didn't require too much effort. In those days, it did not. Who would have thought that the Honda franchise someday would be far more valuable than the Pontiac or GMC franchises? At the time of the sale, Lester was selling monthly 300 to 400 Pontiacs, 125 GMC trucks and about 20 Hondas. In any event, it only took a few days for us to become a fully authorized Honda dealer.

That was fortunate because it wasn't long before Hondas became so hot that a dealer couldn't supply his demand, This change was evident around the country in 1979, following (1) the Arab Oil Embargo of the seventies and our increasing dependency upon oil from the Muslim world, (2) the Shah of Iran being exiled and (3) Khomeini returning to Iran from France while leading an Islamic revolution. Not only was this shattering the stability of the oil situation, it also led to the takeover of the American Embassy in Tehran. From then on, the demand for Japanese fuel efficient cars was staggering. We had people intercepting Honda transports arriving at the dealership, climbing on to the transport trucks to see if the serial number of the Honda we had sold them was on the truck. We had to change making specific vehicle sales to customers prior to delivery, and institute a drawing of names of the next customers in line for cars after they were unloaded by the carrier on our premises to prevent potential injury to our customers. It was wild. Fortunately for us, during the period between our updating of the Honda franchise and Khomeini's actions, we had taken every Honda offered to us. We then had about three acres of the little cars on a back lot. Lester Goodson had mentioned by chance on one occasion following the sale that he had once turned down an allocation of cars from Honda and thereafter was always limited to about twenty a month. We had decided in view of the world situation, we would never turn down Honda allocations. Thereafter, every time other dealers in our area would turn down an allocation of cars because they were then difficult to sell, we would take the cars. I must admit we were just about at the point of reconsidering this policy, having over three hundred of them in stock, at the time Khomeini's shenanigans rendered the problem moot.

By 1980, we had sold all the El Paso dealerships to local dealers there; and J. T. Gilbert and Fred's son both joined us in Houston, as they had been managing the El Paso dealerships since Fred left for Houston. It was also in 1980 that we bought our second dealership in Houston. On Interstate 45 North just less than two miles from the Goodson deal was a large Chevrolet operation, McMahon Chevrolet. It was in financial trouble through excessive borrowing with floating interest rates. About the time their mortgage and floor plan interest rates reached 20 percent, its annual operating net income of just less than two million dollars had been exceeded by *other deductions* of interest and repossessions exceeding that figure. The dealership was placed in bankruptcy. We thought the deal had real potential and now J.T. Gilbert was available to manage it, if we could buy it free of creditor claims out of bankruptcy. I immediately thought of Miron "*Micky*" Sheinfeld, a Houston lawyer specializing in bankruptcy and creditor's problems. I had crossed swords with him in several El Paso cases and was of the opinion that he was highly qualified in this specialized field. With his guidance, we became a bidder, among others, to purchase the dealership's assets out of bankruptcy, including its Chevrolet car and light-duty truck franchise. There were so many current and contingent liabilities of the dealership that the only safe way to buy the deal was out of bankruptcy. The dealer had made several attempts to sell it before he took bankruptcy, but all had failed. Apparently, the prospective buyers had not considered that they could make a deal contingent on the dealership filing for bankruptcy and the bankruptcy court's subsequent approval of the sale. This would have given a prospective buyer an inside track.

After a lot of preliminary jockeying, it looked like there were at least three serious bidders. We examined the bid proposal and saw only one major obstacle. The successful bidder would have to buy all of the defunct dealership's leases of cars and trucks to customers, which leases were held as security by a local bank. They were almost completely undefined in the proposal—the burden being on the bidders to investigate them. We decided the only safe way to proceed was to go to the bank and examine each lease. We took our used car manager at Goodson and J.T. Gilbert with us and proceeded to the bank. There we found boxes of leases, and also discovered that in addition to leased cars and trucks, there were also leases covering pole trailers, portable sheds and small buildings. What a mess! We also discovered that no other prospective bidder had taken the trouble and time to inspect the leases. We did our best to put a value on each lease of a car or truck. Then, since we were clueless as to the value of pole trailers, portable sheds and buildings, we put a zero value on them to complete our analysis. We did not have enough time to refine our valuation of the non-motor vehicle leases. But from what we saw, we concluded that there was not more than a quarter of a million-dollar loss in the car and truck leases. Relative to the overall opportunity the deal presented, this was not a problem. If our quick inspection, which took about two days to complete, was off by 100 percent, the deal was still a good one. In addition, we really did not believe that the pole trailers and small building leases would be a complete loss. We then focused on what we were willing to pay for the entire deal including the potential loss on the leases. At the bankruptcy hearing for reception of bids, we appeared with our attorney, Mickey Sheinfeld. There was only one other bidder by then, and it was a powerful consortium backed by the family of a former South American dictator. They also had an inside track with Chevrolet, since their proposed dealer-operator had been a roommate of a Chevrolet executive at Notre Dame in their college days. General Motors was not technically a party to the proceeding, although their franchise was at stake. The bids were opened by the bankruptcy judge and we were the successful bidder. The difference in bids was almost exactly the difference in the value we placed on the leases. The other bidder had apparently allowed nothing for them, since they had not bothered to examine them.

Knowing that Chevrolet would not be a happy camper due to the personal relationship mentioned and also because General Motors had been trying in recent years to prevent chain GM dealers from expanding and becoming too powerful. It made the larger dealers harder for GM to control. In view of this, I took Mickey aside and told him we needed to put some heat on GM right then in the initial order of the court approving the sale. We did not have time to take this case to the Texas Motor Vehicle Commission, as the dealership was losing customer good will each day. Its service department was COD with all parts suppliers, and customer cars were sitting around the shop with no parts to repair them. General Motors Acceptance Corporation, the floor plan provider, had a full-time employee on the dealership premises, and they would not release a title to a sold car until the dealership paid it off. Since GM was not a party to the bankruptcy hearing, we decided to request the bankruptcy court to include a provision in its order approving the sale that would declare time was of the essence to quickly close this transaction in order to preserve the dealership's good will. Consequently, we asked that the court *order* Fred Schneider to present the required GM application to become a Chevrolet dealer to the Chevrolet zone office by 12 noon on the Monday following this Friday hearing, and that Fred be further ordered to return to the court with the new dealer sales and service agreement in hand and executed by Chevrolet no later than the following Friday at 12 noon. It also ordered Fred to give the zone office a certified copy of the court order. The judge granted all of the above.

We had already prepared the lengthy GM application together with all attachments, such as the experience of the dealer-operator and evidence of how the deal was to be paid for. We also had the certified court order in hand before we left the court on the day of the hearing. Fred immediately called the zone manager of Chevrolet and asked for an appointment with him first thing Monday morning due to the urgency of the matter. The Chevrolet zone manager had already heard that the factory patsy had not been the successful bidder. The zone manager told Fred that it would be weeks before he would have anytime to talk to him, as Chevrolet was in the middle of recontracting all their dealers in the zone. He also told Fred not to call him, but that he would call Fred when he had time to talk to him.

Regardless, Fred dutifully presented himself first thing Monday morning at the zone office and asked to speak to the zone manager. About this time, the zone manager had seen Fred and came storming out of his office. He asked Fred if he was crazy or something; and if he had the ability to understand plain English. He then invited Fred to leave until the *king* summoned him to come back. Fred said he guessed he had no choice, but he told the zone manager he was under court order to leave his GM application and a certified copy of the court order with the zone manager. Fred also suggested that before he refused to accept them, he might want to take a few minutes to check with the GM legal department about court orders and the like. He reluctantly took the papers, took one look at the court order and the requirement that Fred had to return to court on Friday of that week with the signed Chevrolet papers. He mumbled, "That would never happen and the goofy judge who signed the order must have been smoking marijuana." He then turned and went back to his office, yelling at Fred to remove himself from the premises. Fred did. As soon as Fred returned to the office and told me this story, the telephone rang and the zone manager asked in a sugar sweet voice if it would be possible for Fred to come back to his office at once. Fred did and was welcomed by the zone manager who must have received an *attitude adjustment* pill from GM legal, especially if the zone manager shared with legal his comments about the bankruptcy judge. I knew of several instances in Texas where GM had recently been in recent trouble with bankruptcy courts. Fred and the zone manager attended to some additional paper work. The zone manager told Fred that even though he had done his part to accommodate the deal, it would be impossible to have the signed documents, even if approved by the general sales manager of Chevrolet, back in time for Fred's court date on Friday. He also correctly stated that since Fred would become a GM chain dealer in the event of approval, the whole file had to go first to GM headquarters and then to Pontiac for its approval. Fred opined that he hoped the zone manager was mistaken about the time it would take to do all this as he dreaded appearing in court on Friday empty handed.

We heard nothing until Fred got a call from the zone manager at 8:30 AM on that Thursday. The zone manager said, "Congratulations, Mr. Schneider, you have just become our newest Chevrolet dealer." He then asked Fred to come to his office and pick up his dealer sales and service agreement. Chevrolet had decided to leave nothing to chance that Fred would miss his Friday deadline due to its failure to approve the sale and issue the franchise. As I told Mickey Sheinfeld, "It is amazing how fast things move, if you light the right fire under the right behind." What was equally interesting was that the court order was directed at Fred, not General Motors. I suppose their legal department knew that, but was confident the next order they saw if they blew Fred off would have their name on the front page. They would have been correct in that analysis, but the sad fact was the process would have taken more time than we had. It was imperative that we get our arms around this dealership and its numerous problems quickly.

We named the new dealership *Landmark Chevrolet Corp.* This name was suggested by Ruskin Smith's wife, and we liked it best of those we considered. We operated the dealership and made it successful. We restored its customer satisfaction level from a 58 rating to one in the high 80s. We could never get as many Chevrolets as we could sell, as the same zone manager was there the entire time we owned the dealership. In fact, he sent us a letter in the summer of 1984 advising that due to the diverse market area in which we were located, Chevrolet could not allocate nor should we expect to receive any cars or trucks resulting in the dealership having at any time in the future more than several hundred grounded units. The former dealership, which had been owned by a former Chevrolet regional manager who took it into bankruptcy, had never had that kind of restriction, as he regularly sold some four hundred units a month and always maintained a large grounded inventory. A dealer has to have a large inventory for customer selection when he expects to sell that many units a month. While the ink was still wet on the zone manager's letter, we were contacted by a large Chevrolet chain dealer who said he would like to buy the dealership. We told him that everything we owned but our wives and children was for sale. He came to Houston and brought an accountant with him that told us how smart and great he was. We didn't want any potential buyers in the dealership during working hours, so Fred and I walked the two of them through that night. We had already told them what it would take to buy the deal. The accountant claimed he could just walk through the dealership in a short time, mentally appraising its furniture, equipment and other fixed assets as he went. That seemed to be the only item that they had a question about in our pricing, so we obliged them. The accounting expert cut his walk short as a guard dog nearly took the seat of his pants out when he got too close to a security fence. Afterwards, Fred and I agreed to meet with the potential buyer and his exalted accountant-fixed-asset appraiser at 8:30 AM the following day. Fred and I had a late dinner on the way home. We decided we wouldn't sell toilet paper to the dealer as long as he had this *expert* involved in the transaction. But we were curious to hear the results of his walk through appraisal the following morning. We were sitting on the edge of our seats at 8:30 AM; and then we asked the expert how much they thought the fixed asset price should be. He answered with some amount approximating $176,000. The former dealer had a fire just a short time before taking bankruptcy, and had purchased a lot of new-replacement equipment. They had almost-new parts bins that alone cost over $250,000. With that we told both the dealer and the expert to hit the road as we did not want to sell the deal. The dealer had not seen it coming and almost had a stroke. He sent the expert out to his car to wait for him, and then explained that he had never laid eyes on the gentleman before the previous morning when he picked him up at the expert's home base in the dealer's airplane. He begged us to continue negotiations with him without his expert. We refused, and he reluctantly left the store.

The hook was set. Essentially, he had been told that he could not buy the deal. It's amazing what psychological forces are set into motion when someone wants to buy something and can afford it, but is told he cannot have it at any price. We must have received twenty calls from him over the next several months asking us to reconsider. He had some mutual friends call for him to vouch that he was a qualified buyer. Now the hook was in his gut. Finally, we decided to reel him in and *reluctantly* told him we would entertain the thought of renewing negotiations. He quickly informed us that he was not going to bring the accountant, but instead his lawyer. We told him to please do that as we felt he would need some good legal representation if we had any chance to make a deal. He and his attorney came to Houston within several days. The dealer sat in Fred's office with him, and his attorney and I chatted in my office. I told him what it would now take to buy the deal, which was about one million dollars more than we first offered to take. He was very pleasant, and after we had told a few jokes and discussed a number of details, he asked whether I would draw the papers or should he return to his hometown and prepare them. I told him that if he and his client would stay overnight, I would prepare a contract that we would be willing to sign by 1 PM the following day. When we announced to Fred and the principal that his attorney and I had agreed on terms, the principal said that he was disappointed because he thought there would be a big explosion between us and he wanted to see it. No such luck!

We made the deal with them; and the purchase price was over three and one-half times what we had paid for the deal in bankruptcy. Not a bad return in less than four years. The deal was closed in my office soon thereafter. The dealer and his attorney brought the top organizational man from Chevrolet's headquarters with them to the closing. It went smooth, and in leaving the Chevrolet executive told the purchaser that he guessed it was about time to tell the zone manager that a deal in his zone had changed hands. Off they went. This tells you a lot about the clout this purchaser had with Chevrolet, because I had never heard of any deal being closed without the zone manager's knowledge. In less than two weeks following the closing, a motorized transport convoy with Chevrolet cars and trucks galore started streaming into the dealership. When the smoke cleared, there were over two thousand grounded units at the dealership. They must have been assembled just outside the city limits of Houston. As I mentioned previously, the ink was hardly dry on the zone manager's letter telling us the Chevrolet allocation system would not provide more than several hundred grounded units for this location. The dealership soon became the largest Chevrolet retail sales outlet in the world, and as far as I know, it still is. Regardless, we were happy as it had been a very successful investment for us. Like Lester Goodson, we wanted everyone to be happy with the deal and especially us. Frankly, nobody else in the world would have paid our price at that time.

Shortly after the Landmark sale, we heard a rumor that one of the other Honda dealerships in the city might be for sale. I called one of the owners of Spring Branch Honda early the next morning and told him Fred and I would like to meet with him and his partner that day. He told us to come over that afternoon, and we did. The rumor had been true and we took dead aim right at the target, as the Honda dealership had the largest planning potential for the Houston area. Honda was pressing the dealer to build a new facility, as their present location at Bunker Hill and Interstate 10 contained only thirty-one thousand square feet of land and twenty-one thousand square feet of building. They could not face the problems of acquiring new land, building a new building and then disposing of the existing facility after moving to the new one. When we left at 5:30 PM that day, we had a handshake deal to purchase the deal and its real estate. I was going to draw the contract the next day, which was a Wednesday, and send them and their attorney copies of the agreement by 2 PM that day; and then we agreed to meet in their attorney's office at 9 AM on Thursday to sign the deal.

All of this happened as agreed, except the signing of the deal. When Fred and I got to their attorney's office Thursday morning, they left us cooling our heels for almost an hour in the waiting room. Finally, we were invited into their attorney's office and conference area. The principals of the dealership were sitting around the conference table along with their accountant and attorney. Without inquiring into the reason for the delay, I asked the attorney if he had found any objection to the sales documentation. He then assumed a highly aggressive attitude and informed us that the deal was off because the offered price was inadequate. We inquired of the principals about what happened to the number we discussed and shook hands on. One hung his head and the other laid his face down on the table. There was no reply from either. The attorney said that we might as well leave and his face was bright red. We expressed our surprise and disappointment at this revolting turn of events. We asked for some indication of what we might have done to warrant this treatment. About this time, one of the principals spoke out that he just couldn't stand it any longer and he had to tell us what had happened. He said that after we had left their offices on Tuesday afternoon, he remembered that he had to call a Honda dealer in Dallas who was a member of his *Dealer 20* group (twenty dealers from different markets who sell the same product that meet together to learn from each other); he recalled that he had promised if they decided to sell their deal, to call him *first*. Having failed to do that, he called him *second* and told him our proposed deal. The Dallas dealer offered him $500,000 more for the dealership and real estate. Fred and I excused ourselves for several minutes to discuss the problem. We agreed that (1) we were not going to engage in a bidding war with anyone and (2) we would meet the price if the owners would sign the contract with us now. We returned to the table with that proposition, reminding them that we had all agreed on the lesser figure after several hours of discussion. In view of that, we told them that the only fair thing to do was to accept our final offer for $500,000 more and sign the contract without further delay. They accepted and then the meanest lawyer I had ever met became one of the nicest and most accommodating. We made a few changes to the deal and all parties signed it. We left the attorney's office and called the Honda zone manager in Dallas and told him what we had done. He said that it would take some time to secure the formal written approvals from his superiors in California; however, if we were willing to commit to a new facility acceptable to Honda, he recommended that we proceed and close with them as soon as possible, and let the formal approvals come in due course. This was only the first step in nailing down Honda's approval, but it was more than we did when we did not even call anyone at Honda about our purchase of Lester Goodson. This deal was too good to take any chance that it might get away from us. The following Monday was Labor Day, 1984; and over the preceding Friday, Saturday and Sunday, we took inventory and made the necessary adjustments to the purchase price that resulted from the physical count of various inventories and then closed the transaction on the Tuesday following Labor Day. For some time thereafter, if we needed a lawyer who could be mean on cue we used the one who had represented the sellers in this transaction.

It was also in the early 1980s that we met Malcolm Bricklin. Malcolm had grown up in California and at the ripe old age of twenty-one had inherited his father's hardware business. He soon sold it for a million dollars. Full of youth, adventure and trust, Malcolm took a promissory note from the purchasing corporation. When payment was due, the maker defaulted; and Malcolm found it had previously transferred all its assets to some other entity, leaving the purchasing company who gave Malcolm the note defunct. Chances were that the transfers could have been set aside or voided as fraudulent as to creditors, but Malcolm did not pursue the matter. Instead, he moved on to other opportunities and remembered that he had seen a lot of Japanese cars at the dock area that we not been cleared by customs. This was in the late 1960s. He went to the customs office and inquired as to the problem, and they told him why the cars had not been cleared. Malcolm (he had long hair and was a hippy at this time) got on an airplane and went to Japan. He walked into the headquarters of Subaru Motors (although the name may have been different at that time) and asked to see the *boss*. He was ignored. Every day he would come back to their offices, ask to see the boss and hang out there all day. Finally, after nearly a week, someone less than the boss asked him what he wanted. He told them that they had cars stacked up on the U.S. West Coast that could not be cleared by customs without his help. Seeing the Subaru employee was somewhat surprised that this hippy young American had such information, Malcolm pressed on with his wonderful gift of gab. Since he knew no Japanese and the employee knew little English and no *hippyese*, about all he understood to take back to his superiors was the fact that this young man knew of their customs problem in the States and claimed he could fix it. The executives decided to give Malcolm an audience, and since he could sell snowballs to an Eskimo, Malcolm convinced them that he knew some secret that would get their cars into the United States market before they were consumed by rust. When asked what he wanted out of it, Malcolm told them *not much* and no money. All he said he wanted, in the event he was successful with customs, was an exclusive distributor's agreement to import Subarus into the United States and Hawaii. There was considerable argument about Hawaii, but they finally agreed.

They signed some sort of Japanese agreement that purported to document the deal. Malcolm went back to California and immediately went to the customs office he had first visited. He asked them to tell him exactly what he had to do to clear customs with the cars in port. They told him, and he proceeded to follow their instructions to the letter. The cars cleared customs. This is how Malcolm relates that he brought Subaru into the United States. Of course, he had lined up capital partners by then. He also relates that he came up with Subaru's initial slogan in the United States, *One-Two-Subaru.* In some sort of a financial arrangement, he sold his interest to his capital partners along the way, apparently taking the proceeds to Canada to build his dream car, the *Bricklin*, a sports car with gull-winged doors. He manufactured a number of these cars in Canada and sold them primarily in the United States. All went well, until his politics went awry. Apparently, Malcolm had fallen out with the labor minister of the province in which he was operating and with his borrowing source in the United States which forced the company into bankruptcy. At the time of his company's demise, Malcolm's mother was handling all warranty matters and customer complaints from her kitchen.

Fred and I met Malcolm at the suggestion of Karl Singer, a mutual friend. We went to New York and Malcolm and his staff met us in offices loaned to him by someone who owned a lot of New York landscape and had backed Malcolm in past ventures. The meeting was bottomed on the fact that Fiat, the Italian car manufacturer, had recently withdrawn from the United States market. Among Fiat's former offerings were two sport cars, one a spyder-type convertible, designed by Pinafarina and the other a targo-top coupe designed by Bertone, both design studios located in Turin, Italy. Malcolm had signed with them to become the exclusive importer of these two cars in the United States, as both design studios stood to lose a lot of investment because Fiat withdrew from the United States market. Malcolm had a skeleton organization in place and had made financial arrangements with the two design studios, which in turn had an arrangement with Fiat to manufacture the cars as they had in the past but under the brand names of *Pinafarina* and *Bertone* respectively. Malcolm told us that he wanted to offer us the opportunity of being the distributorship for the Gulf States region.

All we had to do was to capitalize a separate company as the distributorship and put up a letter of credit of about eight million dollars to secure the letter of credit his import company had given to the Italians. The trouble with a letter of credit is that it is irrevocable in normal circumstances. Our only protection was that it could only be drawn upon by the presentation to our bank of an *original* purchase order for cars signed by our distributorship. We looked at the numbers with Malcolm and were impressed by the fact that if the distributorship network sold only 50 percent of the same cars that Fiat sold in the United States its last year in business, there was a tremendous amount of money to be made. In fact, it looked so good at the time given the past demand and sales history of these cars, that Fred and I ignored one of our adopted corporate mottos: *the pigs get fat and the hogs get slaughtered*. We talked Malcolm into also giving us the distributorship for the West Coast where import penetration was about 70 percent of the total car market.

Between the West Coast and Gulf States regions, this would account for almost 50 percent of Malcom's total potential sales in the United States. Of course, it also meant that we would have to form another separate company for the second distributorship and put up an additional eight-million dollar letter of credit. The deal on paper looked almost as good as one first looked when a group of El Paso businessmen, including Fred, our banker's son, another car dealer and a Mexican national business tycoon, purchased a 50,000-watt clear-channel radio station situated in Mexico. But that is a whole different story.

After the deal with Malcolm was signed and Texas Commerce Bank issued our irrevocable letters of credit, we formed our two distributorships and hired two people with automobile wholesale experience to be our general managers in the two regions. One had been a Ford Motor Co. regional manager and he was to undertake the Gulf States assignment. The other was an old Pontiac friend, who had been assistant zone manager in Dallas, Texas, and was then the Pontiac zone manager in Los Angeles. Both men were familiar with many dealers in their respective regions. Our distributorships then began signing dealer sales and service agreements with quality dealers in both regions. Fred and I took Malcolm with us to see Bank of America in California in order to hopefully establish a source of floor plan credit for our dealers in the West region. He brought along a friend whose name I do not remember, but he was the producer of *Mr. Mom*, a popular movie at that time. Bank of America had been burnt on dealer floor plan when Fiat pulled out of the United States, and nobody gave us much of a chance to commit them to a floor plan arrangement for former Fiat automobiles. But the bank official was so charmed by Malcolm and *Mr. Mom* that it was a relatively easy sell. We next took Malcolm with us to Houston to attempt to establish a floor plan line with Texas Commerce Bank. However, this was not as imperative as most of our Gulf States dealers had their own sources of floor plan credit. In any event, our bank officers had a good time visiting with Malcolm. With these details accomplished, we were ready in record time to start doing business and to, of course, take in the huge potential profits.

Surprise and danger signal #1: During the Houston trip, Malcolm mentioned that the first cars from Italy would be going to the Mid-East Region. We asked why? Import penetration in that area was among the lowest in the country and especially was this true with convertibles and targo-top coupes. Malcolm said that he owed it to the distributor of that region, who had backed him in the Bricklin car venture. We were very concerned to hear that the success of the venture was dependent on the introduction of the cars on the East Coast and then proceeding westerly until it reached our Gulf States region and finally to the West Coast region. Bear in mind that our two regions represented almost 50 percent of the forecasted sales for the United States. Moreover, the cars would be easier to sell on the West Coast with its 68-70 percent import market penetration. Even the Gulf States region, which would be getting cars before the West Coast region under Malcolm's plan, had only about a 30-35 percent import market penetration at that time. Accordingly, we told Malcolm that it made more sense to us, not only because of our stake in the venture, but also for the venture's overall success, to start with the West Coast region where these cars had done well as Fiats and then work back to the East Coast. Conversely, if the cars flopped in the east, by the time we had cars to sell in the west, they would be introduced with bad trade press for their poor showing in the east. But Malcolm had a history of loyalty to past backers. He was blind to the risk and high on the deal or something, and his headquarters were located in the east.

Surprise and Danger Signal #2: Both Fred and I made two separate trips to Italy to work with the design studios and heard more things that were concerning to us. Meeting with Pinafarina and Bertone separately revealed how different the two were. Pinafarina was an aristocrat; and during this period of unrest with the Red Brigade, he always drove a small inconspicuous car and was accompanied by a small army of security guards with submachine guns in other vehicles. At dinner, he would rent the entire restaurant and the guards were at every entrance. Bertone, on the other hand, was considered a man of the people. He would take us to dinner in a restaurant filled with ordinary Italians. He would arrive by himself driving a Ferrari model he had designed. It was quite a contrast in style and thinking. Bertone displayed his entire car museum to us. Some of the cars were fifteen to thirty years old and still looked futuristic to us. It was a fantastic experience, as he allowed the distributors and their wives to crawl in and over these beautiful museum pieces. Pinafarina did not show us any products from his extensive museum when we visited his studio.

At meetings with each, the reaction and cooperation was quite different. This was particularly apparent on the second trip to Italy when I went to represent our interests. By that time, the East Coast introduction was not going well; and it was necessary to get the two studios to agree to reduce the flow of cars until they started selling better or we would bury the East Coast dealers with product and use up a large portion of Malcolm's letter of credit to the Italian designers. Pinafarina flatly refused, but Bertone agreed to reduce the allocations temporarily. Pinafarina had other fish to fry at this time, as he had landed a contract with General Motors to design and build the body of the forthcoming Cadillac Allante sports car. Bertone, on the other hand, was largely dependent at the time on the successful launch of the Bertone in America.

I also found out during the meetings on this trip that Malcolm's representative with the design studios was complaining about quality problems on the cars being produced for the design studios at the Fiat plant. Maybe Fiat still meant *Fix It Again Tony*. I was also surprised that the cost per car was rising significantly due to changes Malcolm had told his *fix it* man to authorize. It appeared, for example, that most of the cars were being ordered with leather and other expensive cosmetic changes. Our forecasted sales analysis had been based on prices only slightly higher than Fiat's when they sold them in the United States. Due to the large number of changes that had been ordered on the cars, we could not find anybody in Malcolm's or the design studios' organizations that could tell us the final price of the new cars currently being produced.

Surprise and Danger Sign #3: Whenever cost was mentioned in our distributors' private meetings in Italy, Malcolm kept saying, "Don't worry about the cost of the car, we'll just increase the retail price of the car." The trouble with this approach is that the greater the retail price of the car, the more questionable the original sales projections based on a modest price increase to the Fiat version became.

The next result of the second trip to Italy was that Fred and I decided that these surprises and danger signs equaled strike three for our involvement in Malcolm's deal. Shortly, thereafter we met with him and offered to sell back to his company the two distributorships for a modest profit plus the return of all of our *original* purchase orders for cars. Since the letters of credit our bank issued to his company were irrevocable for one year, the only way we could protect ourselves was to get back the *original* purchase orders we had already given Malcolm, as they were the only trigger to anyone drawing on our letters of credit. To the extent they were not drawn upon, they would expire after the one-year term. Malcolm agreed to this arrangement, and we closed the sale of the two distributorships as soon as we had our original purchase orders in hand. We met him in California to accomplish the latter, and he handed them over. On the airplane back to Houston, we examined them in detail and noticed that they were signed by us in black ink. Then we spent the next hour holding the signature pages of the orders up to the airplane windows trying to determine if in fact they were *originals* or just copies. We finally concluded that they were the originals. Fred and I mutually pledged to each other never to sign an important document again in black ink. That in itself is a worthwhile lesson to be learned. With today's copiers, it is even more important as I have seen copies of original documents that look as authentic as the originals. Subsequently, Malcolm's entire empire once again unfortuntely landed in bankruptcy.

You can never keep a good man down, and *Teflon* Malcolm always seemed to land on his feet. His next project was the ill-fated introduction of the Yugo, a low-priced car made in Yugoslavia. We turned down an offer of a distributorship on these cars, but we did agree to become a dealer. The opportunity did not last long, as we were experiencing about four engine failures in every ten car sales shortly after their delivery. We decided on our own slogan *Yugo, we go.* The last we heard from Malcolm, he was at the National Automobile Dealer Association meeting in Las Vegas; and he was attempting to sign up auto dealers in attendance to sell his latest toy, an electric bicycle. He even gave us a demonstration ride inside of a large gym-like structure. He told Fred and me that he had purposely saved the Florida distributorship for the bicycles especially for us. We thanked Malcolm for thinking of us again, but passed. He then offered to sign up each of our dealerships for a franchise to sell the bikes. Even though less risky, we also passed this well-meaning offer. After all, you cannot hog all the good deals for yourself; you must leave something for others to do. Several Houston dealers signed up, but this franchise also had a short history.

After escaping that fate, we purchased in 1985 an Oldsmobile dealership in Winter Park, Florida (the only one in the greater Orlando area). It did not take long to discover that the books of the existing dealership must have been kept by *Mickey Mouse* and also that the rent car companies in Orlando could buy new Olds cars for less than its dealers. Many of these had sales outlets larger than the car dealerships, and many of the new cars were sold by them instead of renting them for a minimum period of time as technically required under GM fleet policies in effect at the time. It did not seem that Oldsmobile Division, whose cars were red hot at the time, had very much interest in policing the rent car policy violations. The next thing we discovered was that the only Olds dealer in Fort Lauderdale had just been awarded the second point in Orlando. We protested this and soon discovered why he was the largest Olds dealer in the United States at the time. We subpoenaed the allocation records for the zone in the protest case; and found that each March or early spring, Oldsmobile Division allocated his dealership in Fort Lauderdale hundreds of extra cars for a *one-day* sales event. Those car sales were factored into the dealer's travel rate and perpetuated his allocation of cars for most of the year. For the following years that we examined, Olds would give him the same *spring booster allocation*, and he would be reloaded to maintain his number-one status nationally. Now, Olds wanted to introduce him to Orlando.

We didn't wait for the outcome of our protest to his second point; and we also decided that we didn't want any more of this action in the gateway to Disney World. We had an opportunity to sell the dealership to a chain operation—Key Royal Auto Group, headquartered in Birmingham, Alabama—for a profit, and we did. They were represented in the sale by the same lawyer as the one who represented the buyer in the 1984 sale of Landmark Chevrolet in Houston. It was coincidental that we had renamed the Oldsmobile dealership *Landmark Oldsmobile*.

We filed suit against the former owner for damages due to what we felt had been a breach of the warranties in his contract with us, and which dealt with his dealership's financial statements. The former principal was hard to find to serve with suit papers, as he had more or less retired on his yacht and was somewhere in the Caribbean. We contacted numerous people working around the major docks in the Virgin Islands to report any sightings of him. Ironically, his yacht was named *Follow Me*. We tried but didn't secure service of the suit papers on him until we received a tip that he was coming back to his apartment in Orlando for a short stop. We served process on him at that time, and immediately took his deposition before he vanished again. Ultimately, we settled the case as it was too costly and impractical to pursue the case in Florida after we no longer had a presence there.

In 1986, we opened an Acura store in Irving, Texas across the street from the Dallas Cowboys' stadium. It was one of the first fifty Acura franchises awarded in America. Unlike some, it was profitable from the beginning as it was well located, and we had the advance opportunity to train the personnel that would operate it in our Houston stores. It has often been the sales leader for Texas, and is usually in the top four or five Acura stores nationally in sales volume. The dealership was also one of most profitable dealerships in the nation, and it has also been recognized for its splendid record of customer satisfaction. Its president is Clark Richardson, Fred's son-in-law. He had trained for the job in our Goodson Honda store in Houston. He learned well.

In 1987, Houston experienced an economic downturn like it had never experienced when the oil business slumped. The words *layoffs* and *boom town goes bust* were daily employed by the media. Actually it was good training opportunity for automobile dealers in Houston where business had been so good over the years that many dealers did not have a clue about how to react in a down market. We looked at our situation, and taking a worse case scenario, we felt we could weather any financial storm likely to continue for the next year or two by cutting our payroll. We talked with our key people and decided the fairest way to take this bitter pill was by cutting current pay levels of all employees by 10 percent and executive pay by 35 percent, in order to avoid layoffs. This strategy worked well and permitted us to retain our people without any layoffs as long as the downturn lasted. We did not lose a person because of the pay cut. Things got better by late 1988, and we were off with a flying start in 1989 with our employees pay almost back to normal.

Probably during this period, our bank understood our operation for the first time. Even though we owned our facilities (with mortgages), each dealership paid market value rent on their property to a non-operating division of the dealership or to the nonoperating division of Lester Goodson Pontiac, d/b/a Goodson Honda-Pontiac-GMC, which owned its own facilities and those of Goodson Spring Branch Honda. In any case, the bank became aware of the fact that not a dime of profit appeared on our financial statements until the rent had been paid, and the nonoperating division of the applicable dealership paid all our mortgage obligations from the rentals received. Before this period, most of our bankers seemed to assume that we made the mortgage payments out of the profit they saw on our statements. Thereafter, we did not hear again the old banking adage about lending to a *single-purpose* customer. In the meantime, all the banks and lending institutions who revered office building loans, which were deemed *multiple purpose* in their minds (leased not to a single, but to multiple tenants) soon had *see-through buildings* added to their vocabularies. This term, of course, described a number of our office buildings that had few if any tenants to support their mortgage payments. Many went through multiple bankruptcies and bargain basement sales before the economy returned to normal in Houston.

And return it did. Some of the city's brighter minds helped form soon after the outset of the downturn the Houston Economic Development Association. Its job was to bring jobs and diversification to Houston. It was completely separate from the Greater Houston Chamber of Commerce, and it raised money from all of our local businesses, large and small. The association was highly successful in bringing companies and jobs to Houston. Those companies were able to relocate to *see-through buildings* in every sector of the community and there was plenty of housing nearby these regional areas for their employees. Within a year or two, the association was bringing fifty-five thousand to sixty thousand jobs annually to Houston. Even better, the industry diversity of these new corporate citizens varied; and following the downturn, Houston was not nearly as dependent on the oil and gas sector.

In 1987, we also established a management company to be called Great Western Management Corp. It was located in an office building near the Goodson Honda-Pontiac-GMC dealership in Houston. This company replaced Great Western Management & Realty Corp., which had been merged into Lester Goodson Pontiac the previous year. This office location housed the executive officers of the company, including Bill Kalkhoff, our controller. Our first executive secretary was Phyllis Carey. When she retired, several others followed but for short terms. Thereafter, until we sold the business, the executive secretary was Barbara Haynes who was great help to everyone in the office. We also had an insurance manager in this office, and Vicki Krantz was at that job the longest and did an excellent job. Until the company was sold, Bill Kalkhoff's very able assistant was Eileen Svoboda. Jeff Wardwell was the general manager of Goodson Advertising, and he handled all advertising matters for the dealerships managed by Great Western Management Corp.

It was during this period of time that Karl Singer, our finance and insurance consultant, convinced us to set up a meeting with a vendor that Karl' company used to help it hire the right person for the right job. Since we knew our success depended upon bringing on and developing good people, we let Karl make an appointment for Fred and me to meet with Jack Evans who was a licensee of *Predictive Index* in Atlanta, Georgia. Jack met us in New Orleans where we were attending back-to-back events—the Super Bowl and the annual meeting of the National Automobile Dealers Association. Jack came over to our rooms at the Windsor Court, which incidentally is one of my favorite hotels in the world. He asked us to fill out a survey questionnaire consisting of the front and back side of a single-page document. He asked our wives to do the same. The survey only takes five to ten minutes to complete. He took our completed surveys and reviewed them. In short order, he gave us a summary of our personal traits related to what each of us was best qualified to do. We had never met Jack before this day, and it was absolutely amazing what he could tell the four of us about ourselves.

The survey is designed to profile a person in depth as to how he or she will likely perform in a particular job category. It tells you many other things as well, such as how likely the person will follow company policy, their present morale and energy levels and if their real self is so in conflict with a particular type of job that an ulcer could be a possibility. This analysis, completed by a prospective employee in minutes, can be analyzed manually or by computer in a few more minutes so the employer can accurately predict whether the prospect fits the job for which he or she is applying. If not, it will tell you what type of work the person could do. In short, Predictive Index helps the employer prevent putting *a round peg into a square hole*. Fred and I had taken a number of similar tests designed to search out the same type of information; however, some had taken nearly four hours to complete. We had also tried handwriting experts on occasion.

We learned that Predictive Index has been periodically reviewed by professors at the *Harvard Business School* to determine statistical reliability. We were so impressed that we signed up with Jack as soon as we returned to Houston. Jack requires that the principals take the training required to read the surveys, and Fred and I allocated the time to do this as well as require that all of our top managers take the same training as soon as reasonably practical. We required that every person we considered for a position take the survey. Anyone I was to interview would receive a survey from our receptionist upon arrival at our offices, retire to the conference room to answer it, and then return it to our receptionist. She imputed the survey answers in our computer; and within fifteen to twenty minutes after the prospect arrived, he or she was sitting in my office. I would already have reviewed the results, and I knew almost as much about the prospect as he or she did about his or her self. Thereafter, our personnel problems were with the few people someone hired when the survey indicated that they were not suited for the job in question. Fortunately, we seldom disregarded what the survey told us and Predictive Index saved us a lot of grief. In reviewing some of the more difficult results, or to merely confirm what I thought to be true, I found Jack Evans to be good and reliable counsel. To this day, I believe he and his son know more about people than anyone I know. Incidentally, this service is not limited to automobile dealers and is used by many national companies in all types of businesses.

In 1991, we doubled our space in this office location to establish one of the first general accounting offices to provide the accounting services for all of our dealerships. This was also under Bill Kalkhoff's supervision and its office manager was Betty Browning. This management and accounting central office arrangement was very impressive to all of our business contacts, particularly our bankers. We also felt that an extended benefit of managing dealerships this way was the high grade of employee we were able to attract to this very business-like central management and office establishment.

For a number of years during this period of time, I served as the president of the Houston Honda Dealer Association. It handled for years the advertising program provided by funds from American Honda for cooperative advertising in the Houston area. We also conducted an annual meeting during the Christmas season for the top sales persons of our local Honda dealers. We would have a quality celebrity speaker, such as Terry Bradshaw, and provide cash prizes for the sales persons. For several years, I represented our district as its zone dealer council representative. In 1991, I was elected as the Dallas zone representative to the Honda National Dealer Council for a two-year term. In 1991, I was elected by the other dealers of the council to serve as its vice chairman; and the following year, I was elected by the National Dealer Council to be its chairman. I was very busy these two years working on problems that would arise from time to time between Honda and its dealer body. However, the work was very enjoyable and our final meeting in both years was a Hawaii venue. Some of our *work* entailed playing golf with our council members and Japanese executives with Honda.

In 1997, I was elected once more by the zone dealer council to represent it in the National Dealer Council. This was also a two-year term, and a turbulent first one. At the very first meeting, a couple of the dealer representatives had teamed up with the past chairman to amend the existing bylaws to such an extent that dealers would not be electing their representatives to the national council in future years. Instead, these council members wanted committees to replace elected representatives on the council. The initial membership on these committees would be controlled by three individuals who happened to be the last three chairmen of the national dealer council. From that point on, the committees would perpetuate themselves. In other words, the friends of the original clique who dreamed up this device would likely be politically obligated, or at least motivated, to keep the three *founding* individuals involved as long as they wanted to control dealer-Honda relations. I knew from prior experience how politically motivated the ring leader was. He also had been elected to the council by his zone twice, but our council bylaws required a two-year hiatus after serving before you could be elected again. This bylaw provision was in place to discourage anyone from becoming a permanent fixture on the council. It was important to have new blood from time to time. A good council member was one who could lay aside a personal agenda in favor of working with Honda for the benefit of *all* dealers, large or small.

That evening at dinner, I discussed with a few old friends on the council the danger of what was about to be voted on and some had not realized that elected members would be a thing of the past. The clique group had already written a plan to form the basis of new bylaws to establish membership perpetuation through the committee system, but many just glance at legalistic documents and fail to consider all the overall effect. My friends helped us to lead a rebellion against the change, and by the time we voted, we had a majority of the council in place to defeat the proposal. I was chosen to draft new bylaws that would allow committees to be effectively used to increase the quality and frequency of the dealer council's communication with the factory and the dealer body; but these committees would be controlled by the national dealer council and the council membership would still be elected by all Honda dealers as in the past. I drafted the new bylaws over the course of the next few months and had them approved by both Honda and the National Dealer Council. Substantially the same bylaws were also adopted by the separate National Dealer Council for the Acura division.

During my years on the national dealer council, one of the highlights was meeting Soichiro Honda, the founder of Honda Motor Co., Inc. He made a rare visit to the United States shortly before his death on August 5, 1991. The national dealer council and their wives were invited to a dinner in California to honor him. He was what the kids today would call a *hoot.* At the dinner, he traded jackets with a waiter and then served wine to all the dealers and their wives. He was having such a good time that the president and other executives of American Honda had a hard time getting him to agree to go to bed. Maybe that shouldn't have been a surprise to them because when he was seventy-seven, he was still hang-gliding, skiing and ballooning.

During this time period, Fred and our group also bought Honda and Infiniti dealerships in California, as well as a Toyota dealership in Houston but all were ultimately sold when we accepted the fact that we were actually in the *people* business, and there was never a surplus of qualified and honest people to go around. Moreover, we usually found, when we acquired a dealership from someone else, that you could not always count on inheriting a lot of good people in the deal. We simply could not stretch the good managers we already had thin enough to operate successfully eight or nine locations from California to Florida. We reviewed where we were and where we wanted to be. Our conclusion was to reduce the number of dealerships and locations to our Houston and Dallas stores, as we had developed an outstanding staff of people with the help of Predictive Index, who could adequately handle these three dealerships with their five franchises. This decision proved to be a good one, as we raised our overall profitability to its highest level, considerably above the periods when we were operating a number of dealerships from coast to coast.

Timing is everything. I will cite a couple of examples that happened during the general time frame preceding and antecedent to this downsizing move. During most of the years Fred and I were in the car business, we had little need for legal counsel, except in certain special situations like using Mickey Sheinfeld to guide us through the purchase of Landmark Chevrolet in the minefield of bankruptcy complications. Sometimes, we enjoyed the good services of Jack Townsend, a Houston tax lawyer, who would represent us skillfully if we had to appeal an IRS decision or the like. Jack is a class act, and there are times anyone can benefit not only from the skill of a lawyer like Jack, but also from his wisdom. He did us another service when we found ourselves in the wrong place at the wrong time. This resulted from some complicated lawsuits filed in civil courts far from our home base; and in which, contrary to general legal principles, we were faced with *defending* ourselves from baseless but serious allegations by assuming, in effect, the burden of *proving we did nothing wrong.* Sometimes this happens as a practical matter when you go up against a hometown adversary in his home base. Jack introduced us to Larry Finder of the Houston office of Haynes & Boone, a large Dallas-based firm with offices in a number of different cities. Larry is a counselor in every meaning of the word. He suggested that we place this litigation in the hands of one of his partners, Joe Werner of the Dallas office. Joe did a skillful job of navigating us through this litigation to the point that we were finally able to settle both cases for what it would have likely cost to try them, particularly in view of the long-distance nature of the venues. Larry and Joe became not only trusted advisors, but good friends as well. They are also both quality people. For example, hardly a day goes by that Larry does not call on his way home from the office or when he gets back to town from frequent business trips to check on the health of my wife. I never talk to Joe that he doesn't inquire about the same subject. Incidentally, my former partner, Fred Schneider, does the same in spades. The litigation was out of the way about the same time as we had implemented the decision to downsize; in fact, it was a factor in our decision to keep all our future activities within the borders of Texas.

Thus, everything was cool by the time the second timing event occurred. In late 1999, we were contacted by a broker who advised us he was representing United Auto Group, a public company which operates over one hundred twenty-five dealerships in the United States and in a few foreign countries. It is controlled by Roger Penske and his associates in Penske Corp. Most people think of Roger Penske as a former race car driver, and then as the owner of the Penske racing team they see on television in Cart or IRL racing events. Roger is much more than that. What many do not know is that Roger got his start as a Chevrolet dealer in 1965. He had then the opportunity to buy Detroit Diesel from General Motors and did so; however, he had to give up his GM franchise in the deal. He grew from this base, as he was very adept in taking on partners with lots of money. They are called the Penske Capital Partners, and they include banks, public companies and nationally known names. Roger, directly or indirectly, possesses practical control over the United Auto Group.

We took this contact seriously and immediately called our financial consultants, Chase Securities, and asked that they prepare a marketing brochure that reflected the history of our recent operations. After securing a confidentiality agreement with UAG, Chase delivered the document to Penske. In January 2000, Roger, his regional vice president and the broker came to Houston to see Fred and me. We drove them by each of the dealerships as well as a twenty-one acre site we had purchased in Houston to build a new Honda facility to relocate Goodson Honda from its then existing location. He apparently liked what he saw and asked Fred how much money it would take for UAG to purchase all of our Houston dealerships. At that time, we were driving by one of our dealerships on Interstate 10. Just before Roger asked how much money Fred wanted, Fred was turning from his position in the front seat to face Roger in the rear seat. Fred's knee then made contact with the front passenger window switch, which automatically lowered the window on his side, just as Roger asked the *how much* question. Fred's hearing in his left ear is impaired anyway and with the wind whistling in the open window, he only heard the *how much money* part and not the part about for *all the dealerships*. Fred's answer was based upon his assumption that Roger was only talking blue sky. We parted that day with everyone happy with what they understood the deal was, but we were actually many millions of dollars apart.

I suspected that was the case, and when Roger and his group flew off in his airplane, I clarified the matter with Fred. He told me he was only pricing the blue sky. I called the broker the next morning to tell him what Fred had *thought* that Roger had asked. He acknowledged that Roger left with the impression that the price Fred gave him was for all the assets of the dealerships, except real estate. It took several days to hear back, since now we were negotiating from ground zero. However, we soon had another meeting in Houston with the broker and I gave him our audited financials for 1999;

and we discussed a number of major points that we wanted if a deal was to be made. Next, I was invited to Detroit to visit with Roger and his financial advisors about the deal under discussion. After a few hours, I did not feel we were getting anywhere in the ball park of making a deal. I had asked our banker, Curt Karges from Chase Manhattan Bank, to go to Detroit with me, as he knew some of Penske's financial advisors. I whispered to Curt that I was done and we excused ourselves. After we returned to Houston, I called the broker and asked that he return our financials and other documents furnished to them because we were not making any meaningful progress.

The next day I received a call back from him and he assured me Penske and UAG wanted to do a deal. I responded that if that was so, they should make a concrete offer and we would consider it; but we didn't want to waste any more time with ring-around-the-rosy talks. I next received a material term sheet setting forth their offer and the significant points in issue. It resembled a letter of intent, which is not actually binding, but does tend to get the deal moving toward a comprehensive contract. The offer did not contain enough blue sky and had other unsatisfactory terms, including the fact that I would have to stay on with UAG for five years. I marked it up and returned it with our counter proposal. We went back and forth with material term sheets until finally on March 21, 2000, we reached an agreement on the big issues, including price, structure of the transaction and my employment contract for a two-year period.

I immediately contacted our transactional attorney, Arthur Nathan, a senior partner in Haynes & Boone that Larry Finder recommended we use to prepare definitive agreements evidencing the sale of our two Houston dealerships and UAG's agreement to lease the real estate which we were not selling in the deal. UAG had its regional attorney review the finished drafts and suggested several minor changes and one major one. They wanted an escape clause in the event the due diligence review turned up something they felt was adverse. I told them it would be next to impossible to draft a clause like that which we would accept. Instead, I told Roger that if they were satisfied with our documentation after we incorporated their minor changes and if he was willing to execute it without further changes assuming due diligence produced results satisfactory to them, then we would give them up to ten days before either of us signed the documents to do their due diligence work. If they didn't want the dealerships after they completed their due diligence process, then no one was obligated to do the deal. An escape clause, based upon subjective due diligence audits in a contract signed by all parties, had too often been used in the past by large automobile consolidators to raise issues at the closing table. Under the threat of calling off the deal at this critical point, some of these companies allegedly used even minor items to reduce the total purchase price. At that point, the buyer would have the upper hand. Roger said that he understood our point and agreed to our concept of no one being bound until due diligence had been completed to the buyer's satisfaction.

UAG people came to Houston and spent about a week going over all our books of account, agreements to be assumed and other documents. When they were finished they seemed to be happy; and the next day Roger called and said he would come to Houston on May 4 and sign the documents. I met him at the airport, and we went to a nearby hotel conference room and signed the documents. The deal closed without incident after the July 4 holiday, but it took several miniclosings over the next several days following the main closing to allow the old and new floor plan sources to get all their ducks in a row. Obviously, this was the most important deal for me personally that I ever negotiated, and I was happy with the results.We did not sell our Acura deal in this package, as Mr. Penske did not want to enter the Dallas market at that time. The retention of this deal was beyond our expectation, as we had assumed any buyer looking at us would also want this outstanding dealership. It worked particularly well for Fred that this buyer did not, as that would leave Fred a dealership for his son and son-in-law's futures.

I was named as president of all of the Houston subsidiaries of UAG that had been organized to purchase our assets and franchises, and I began the transition from an owner to an employee of a national publicly owned company. That is never an easy transition for an entrepreneur to make. However, all of my future dealings with Roger Penske were without incident. I also began to turn over more duties to my former general manager, Rocky McCullough, who had also stayed with UAG. It was our plan over my two-year term to transfer as much authority as possible to Rocky, as it appeared to everyone concerned that he would be my logical successor. Actually, this transition was accomplished for all practical purposes during the first year or so. At that time, I remained president of Goodson Auto Group for UAG, but I had few other meaningful duties. At the expiration of the two-year term, Roger asked me to stay on for an additional year, but I suggested that we make it month to month. He had told me during the extension period, I could set my own schedule, take care of my wife who was not in good health and be *his eyes and ears in Houston*. After months of being paid only to look and listen, I targeted my seventy-second birthday as a good exit date. Roger agreed that would work for UAG as well.

At the end of the day, it is my sincere hope that Roger Penske and UAG are happy with the entire deal and feel that the purchase was a good deal for them, and that they received some extended benefits from the sellers. There is no other opportunity in the United States to my knowledge where one can acquire two Honda dealerships in one city, as Honda changed its policy permitting the purchase of an existing Honda dealership by another Honda dealer in the same city sometime ago. Moreover, these two dealerships are located in the fourth largest car and truck market in the United States. In this respect,. UAG is a leg up on its competitors. Being a publicly traded company, UAG is in it for the long haul, and it shareholders should benefit substantially in normal economic times.

Later, during a discussion with Fred about my retirement from UAG, he asked me if I would like to sell my interest in our real estate company and in the Acura dealership to him. Since I was the only nonfamily minority shareholder left (our company redeemed J.T. Gilbert's interest at the time of the Penske sale), I agreed that he and I should be the ones to cut such a deal, in order that there would not be an outside shareholder in either company at the time either old soldier just fades away. We reached terms in short order and closed the transaction on November 30, 2002. Thus, my career as an automobile dealer ended. No one could ask for a better partner or friend than Fred, and we are in constant contact with each other by telephone several times a week.

Chapter XIV

NATIONAL LOAN BANK

In the spring of 1987, I received a call from Marc Sharpiro, the vice chairman of Texas Commerce Bancshares, Inc., who advised me that as part of the forthcoming merger between it and Chemical New York Corporation, Texas Commerce had decided not to sell any of their problem loans to Chemical, as it could not receive enough consideration for them in the deal. Instead, he said Texas Commerce planned to form a new national bank, National Loan Bank (NLB), which would be publicly owned by its some thirty-six thousand existing shareholders. Texas Commerce would spin off the problem loans to NLB, whose sole purpose would be to ultimately liquidate the loans to cash for the benefit of such shareholders. Texas Commerce felt this was the best way to realize the maximum value from these problem loans. He then asked me if I be willing to serve as one of the five bank directors and as one of the two bank officers. Since from day one this would be a publicly held company with reporting requirements, we then discussed what means of indemnification existed to protect the proposed slate of directors. He indicated that there would be the usual indemnification provisions in the bylaws of NLB and directors' indemnification insurance provided for them.

Since this was the first *junk* bank in history, and its sole mandate was to liquidate assets that everyone knew consisted of problem loans, it was hard to envision the various risks of serving on its board. Even though these directors would be compensated for attending the board meetings and also receive a modest annual retainer, it would never be compensation commensurable to the risk of being a director of a publicly owned and traded company. I suggested to Marc that I thought that Chemical New York Corporation should also indemnify the directors who were serving their indirect interests by NLB being a vital link in their ability to become the surviving entity in the merger with Texas Commerce. As Marc knew, there are limitations to a public company indemnifying its own directors that can override the indemnification provisions as a matter of public policy. Under the circumstances, I knew of no such limitations to indemnification, except fraud and the like, in a case where a third party like Chemical indemnifies NLB directors. I told him I would be comfortable with that arrangement plus the normal stuff he had in place, and if he could obtain Chemical's agreement, he could count me in. Marc called me back the next day or so, and he told me Chemical had agreed. Thus, I became a director of the NLB, its corporate secretary and bank cashier. The other directors were Harry K. Smith (its chairman), Clayton T. Stone, James W. Robertson and C. A. Watts.

Harry K. Smith had headed his family business, Big Three Industries, since 1948. The company had been co-founded by his father in 1920. Harry had taken the company from being a regional oxygen and nitrogen distribution company to a billion dollar giant in the industry, which among many other things sold liquid nitrogen to NASA's space program. He sold the company to L'Air Liquide, a French company, in 1986. Clayton T. Stone was a real estate expert and had retired as executive vice president of Hines, a worldwide developer of properties in ninety cities in four continents. C.A. Watts was the owner of Arliss Watts Energy/Investments, and before that the president and CEO of North Central Oil Corporation. James W. Robertson was a partner in Liddell, Sapp, Zivley, Hill & LaBoon, a large Houston law firm and counsel for

Texas Commerce Bancshares. It was a very compact and hardworking board. I had always thought that any board of directors with more than three members was suspect; however, my experiences serving on this board over the next seven years changed my thinking upward to a not "more than five" rule.

Our mission was clear but the path we were to travel was uncharted. The Comptroller of Currency just didn't know how to handle a bank, the sole purpose of which was set forth in a Plan of Voluntary Complete Liquidation, pursuant to which, it was to operate from inception to collect or otherwise realize on loans and distribute the net proceeds to its shareholders, not as dividends but as proceeds in partial liquidation. Some of our yield return numbers were over the top, and thus the national bank examiners could only scratch their heads on how to grade performance without wrecking their usual indexes.

On day one, the market placed a value on a share of our stock at about $1.25. We went about the business of collecting loans where we could and foreclosing on them when we could not make significant progress in the time frame we had to do our job and then turn out the lights. Some of our customers had been the elite of the business world in Texas and elsewhere before the energy slump of the mid-1980s. Some significant assets were sold in foreclosure, but it was our policy not to mention the names of our clientele. We actually managed some of the income-producing property in order to pay our expenses, and in the process NLB turned a group of poorly performing miniwarehouse into a cash cow by renovating them and replacing their supervision with competent and honest managers. We kept these storage facilities operating until we were nearing the end of our task as they paid practically all the administration expenses of NLB over its seven-year existence.

As a regulated publicly owned company, we had annual meetings of our shareholders. Because they were getting cash at least once a year or more, not too many of the thirty-six thousand or so shareholders came to the meetings or voted against the directors. I was interested in hearing the few who did attend and in most cases, they were well-meaning people who seemed to want someone to talk to and hear them out. Harry, as chairman, did a good job of politely keeping these types reasonably in line so as not to unduly prolong the meeting for the others who were attending to keep informed.

When we had fully liquidated the loans and sold all remaining tangible assets, we dissolved NLB. There were a number of institutional investors who had asked NLB to stay in business and acquire other problem loans to liquidate for profit. However, we never strayed from our original purpose to liquidate from the outset. When the lights were turned out in 1994, NLB, net of all administrative costs and expenses, had paid out in excess of $5.00 cash per share to its shareholders on liquidating loans that had been worth little to Chemical and only $1.25 per share to the market when we opened the bank's doors without a single depositor.

I take it to be just coincidental that this was the second banking experience with which I had been associated that were historical *firsts*: (1) *Trans Texas Bancorporation*, the *first* bank holding company to be approved by the United States Supreme Court; and (2) *National Loan Bank*, the *first* junk bank in the United States. In both instances, I was simply making the most of opportunities that came my way.

Chapter XV

DIVERSIONS

All work and no play would make anybody dull. We have heard that saying for years. It is easy to say, but not always easy to do. Time and what we do with it is one of life's biggest challenges. The allocation of it creates many conflicts of interest in and of itself. We all know people who carry leisure to an extreme, in that some will put it above family during nonwork hours. Some will put it over family and work. Conversely, we all know people who find no time for leisure and are workaholics by nature. I fall somewhere in between the extremes, as I have never let leisure interfere with work or family; however, I have sometimes let work interfere with family. Fundamentally, in my opinion, I have managed to maintain some degree of balance among these inherent conflicts for the use of my time.

During my law practice days, I devoted some time to sports. It was first tennis because El Paso had an idea climate for it. In addition, I had not been at the law firm very many months until Sidney Rogers, Mr. Hardie's secretary, who had worked for him since she was sixteen years of age, offered me her membership in the El Paso Tennis Club. It was a first-class tennis facility with good courts, a clubhouse and a swimming pool. She would not let me pay her for it, since she and her husband were paying dues but were not then using the club. I willingly accepted their generous offer, and after the usual approval period for transfers of membership, I became a new voting and dues-paying member of the El Paso

Tennis Club. We formed a foursome that played tennis Wednesday nights under lights and on Sunday afternoons. It was composed of Bob Rainbolt, a local heavy truck dealer; Don Studdard, a local attorney with another firm; and Richard C. White, a United States congressman from our district. On occasions when he was in Washington, he had a lawyer friend from Mexico who often filled in for him. The thing I enjoyed about tennis was the fact that you could have a good time as well as a good workout in one and one-half hours. Even playing twice a week did not seem to be an unreasonable loss of family or work time.

After I recovered from the bleeding ulcer in about 1963 following the negotiations with Hertz in New York, my doctor recommended that I switch to golf. He felt it would provide more quality relaxation and would not be as vigorous as tennis. Since he was a golfer of sorts, I do not know his motive in suggesting the change of sports. I had joined Coronado Country Club a year of so before, in order that the kids could have a place to go and swim closer to our home. I made the change, but I never found golf completely relaxing even though it was less strenuous than tennis. I never could understand how an unnatural act like swinging a golf club in such a fashion that results in a straight shot, multiple times during a three to four hour period, would ever be completely relaxing. Nevertheless, I have played golf from time to time since I was three years old. When I played left handed, the best handicap I maintained for any time was seven. After I was nineteen and started playing right handed, the best handicap I maintained while playing at least once on weekends was ten. At the present time, I have not played a game of golf for two or three years, because the sun is my enemy as I am prone to skin cancer probably as a result of sun exposure in my early years.

When I moved to Houston, I never played regularly because in the beginning Fred and I worked twelve-hour days. We also worked Saturdays in the early years. In addition, one never knew if it was going to rain or not on weekends. We did both join Lochinvar Country Club in Houston as it was not too far from our dealerships or the office building in which we worked. We used it primarily for entertaining business guests during the weekdays. It was not close to our homes and so we rarely used it on weekends. During the first twenty years in Houston, I may have played as many as twenty to thirty times a year. During the next four or five years, I probably averaged only eight or ten golf outings annually. As a result, my handicap steadily moved up with my age. But now, I would probably have to be one hundred years old to shoot my age. In the last few years before I quit entirely nearly all of my golf was played in *events* of some sort. For years I played annually in the Honda Classic at the various courses in the Fort Lauderdale area which were its venue at different times. I also played several times in the Shell Houston Open. During my tenure on the Honda National Dealer Council, I played with the other dealers and Honda personnel all over Southern California and several times in Hawaii. The rest of my golf was played in tournaments sponsored by banks, finance companies and sometimes charitable organizations. I also played annually in the Houston Auto Dealers Association tournament. It is difficult to play well in these events with no practice sessions in between. But the fellowship was always great and well worthwhile. The most enjoyable of all my golf outings were those played in the Honda Classic pro-am event with some of the great professional tour golfers of my time. Photos of some of them are included in the appendix to this book.

One of the nicest persons I played with anywhere was Randolph Scott, the Hollywood western actor. This was not in a pro-am event, but what Thunderbird Country Club in Rancho Mirage, California calls a Saturday morning *choose up*. On this day, President Ford, Alan Greenspan and a number of celebrities were present. Randolph Scott was designated to play in my group. For the entire round, all he did was visit with his playing partners wanting to know all about them and what they did for a living. It was impossible to get him to talk about himself. This is rare among the celebrities who frequent the golf courses of the Palm Springs area. Randy was in his early eighties and was long and lanky in excellent physical condition. The only sign that he was that old was the aging skin on his arms visible below the short sleeves of his shirt. In another Saturday *choose up*, Fred and I played with Oral Roberts, the Oklahoma evangelist. He was a very good golfer, and on nearly every putt he attempted, he would first say that he did not intend to leave the putt short "as the good Lord hates a coward." He also explained the money counting machines he employed to receive the enormous mail collections from television listeners. It must have been very substantial as he flew to Palm Springs frequently in his Gulfstream jet. His son then substituted on TV, and he would explain his father's absence to his television flock by saying that Oral had gone to the desert to meditate.

My final story of desert golf experiences has to do with a free putting lesson. I was on the practice green at the same time as Hoagy Carmichael. I had never actually met Hoagy before, although everyone knew who he was and where he lived when he was at this desert resort. His home was near a tough three par at Thunderbird Country Club. When he was in residence, you could tell as there were several very beautiful ladies around his pool. I also knew him as one of our greatest composers of popular songs, including "Stardust," "Georgia on my Mind," "The Nearness of You," and "In the Cool, Cool of the Morning," to mention only a few I now recall. Generally speaking, everyone at Thunderbird left the celebrities to themselves unless they indicated they wanted different treatment. Consequently, I would never have approached Hoagy even though we were the only ones on the green at that time. However, he initiated the conversation, as he had spotted what he felt was a fundamental flaw in my putting grip. He proceeded to show me his grip and then putted six or seven practice holes to demonstrate his accuracy. He suggested that I try his grip and then take several practice putts. I thanked Hoagy for his advice, and I putted so much better that I used his grip for years until I later switched to a cross-handed one.

One of the ironies of life is that one of my good friends is David Feherty, one of the golf commentators on CBS Sports and I have never played a game of golf with him. First off, that fact shows that David is intelligent. Can you imagine what punishment it would be for David to have to watch me hack the golf ball for eighteen holes? David was born and reared in Ireland. He played professionally on the European tour, winning ten tournaments worldwide. He played for the 1991 European Ryder Cup team. His commentary, Irish accent and all, is colorful to say the least. In person and in private, he is still as humorous as when he is doing his television thing. His recent passion is sport and skeet shotgun shooting and he often lugs both his clubs and shotgun with him on trips.

David has arranged for me to watch several recent Shell Houston Open tournaments in the multimillion dollar production trailer of CBS Sports. That is a real treat. It is air-conditioned and beats the heck out of walking the course behind David. Besides you see everything there is to see simultaneously from the numerous monitors in the trailer. Lance Barrow is the head of production. He lives in Fort Worth, Texas, and he is a show himself that is worth the afternoon. He yells at everybody and anyone over their communication headsets. No commentator or cameraman is safe from Lance's critical remarks. On the other hand, praise is only occasional, as professionalism is assumed by Lance. However, something like the near ground view of Fred Couples's winning putt rolling across the green on the eighteenth hole of the 2003 Houston Open drew a word of praise from Lance. I have enjoyed meeting all the CBS commentators as well as many of those who work either in the production trailer or its sister trailer for graphics. David gave me a *CBS Sports* banner (bright yellow and blue) for Father's Day one year, which had been autographed by Lance, David, Jim Nantz and all the other golf commentators. It is a treasured possession and hangs in my hobby room behind our garage. I also keep prized trophies and golf souvenirs in this location, as well as three or four of my old sets of golf clubs.

My wife and I are godparents for David and Anita's five year old daughter, Erin Torrance Feherty. The Torrance is for Sam Torrance, one of David's best friends. Sam was captain of the last European Ryder Cup team. We are also godparents of two of Anita's children by a prior marriage, Fred and Karl Schneider, who are grandsons of my former partner. Consequently, all the Fehertys and Schneiders are like extended family.

David, as a child, had aspirations to become an Irish tenor. But when he found hitting a golf ball was relatively easy for him, he switched to professional golf. After retiring from professional golf to broadcasting, David also became an author. I am sure he has more books in the works, but he has already published *A Nasty Bit of Rough* and *Somewhere in Ireland a Village Is Missing an Idiot.* His writing is as humorous as the words from his mouth. In addition to the golf thing, David is a diversion himself.

Another sports interest developed along the way was professional football. This happened when Fred Schneider had the opportunity to purchase a 10 percent partnership interest in the New Orleans Saints. A group of investors headed by Tom Benson, an automobile dealer in San Antonio, Texas, and New Orleans, Louisiana, purchased the Saints from John Mecom Jr., who decided to sell the team during Houston's downturn in the mid-1980s. From this time until Fred and the other minority owners sold their interests to Tom Benson in December of 1992, we regularly attended most of the Saints' home games and often flew on the team plane on road trips. Early on, one of the interesting trips on the plane occurred when we were sitting in seats just in front of Earl Campbell, the Saints' running back and formerly a Houston Oiler and a Heisman Trophy winner at the University of Texas. Earl was singing "You Are My Sunshine." Archie Manning, who was not then playing but who was on the team's staff, came up the aisle to where we were sitting, and asked us if we knew why they had never made a movie about Earl's life. We confessed we did not know. Archie replied, "Hollywood has not been able to find an actor that sings as bad as Earl." Thinking about it, Archie did seem to have a point.

After Fred sold his interest in the Saints, we leased a suite in the Astrodome and became fans of the Houston Oilers until the owner, Bud Adams, moved the team to Nashville. We had thirty-six seats to fill for each home game to fully utilize our suite. When Bud made his announcement that they were moving, the Oilers had one season left in Houston. Even though we had a suite with food and drink, it was difficult to fill all of our seats by mid-season of that last year. At the end of that season, I ceased active attendance at professional football games. Since then, I watch professional, but mostly college, football in a fifty-yard-line seat in our family media room.

Another diversion of mine is photography. My dad bought me my first camera when I was nine years old, and I have been taking pictures all these years. In the early days, I took color slides. Thereafter, I mostly used color film. Since I turned on a computer for the first time last year, my latest efforts have been with a digital camera. I was very skeptical about digital photography, but it is so versatile that I am completely won over. I seriously doubt if I will use any of my film cameras again. A number of them are already collectibles. Most of the images I take have as subjects—people and places.

That leads me to another diversion that my wife and I share together—*travel.* When I asked her father, Bill Rabb, for her hand, he jokingly (I assumed) told me that if it was anyone but me, he would probably say no. I asked him what he meant by that statement. He laughed and said that Carolyn was always on the go. Bill, before his retirement, had been an international cotton broker. He bought high-grade long staple cotton from the valley farmers in the El Paso and New Mexico areas and then sold it all over the world. He said that Carolyn had gone on some of these trips to Europe with him, and that what he had meant was that she would have me in Europe within a year. That did not seem likely, since at the time I had never been overseas. He was right, however, and we made our first trip to Europe that September. Since then, we have made a number of trips to not only Europe but also to Alaska, Canada, Hawaii, Mexico and the Orient. We have been to Acapulco, Amsterdam, Anchorage, Assisi, Athens, Ephesus, Florence, Frankfurt, Hong Kong, Istanbul, London, Mexico City, Montreau, Munich, Oslo, Paris, Rome, Salzburg, Skagway, Stockholm, Tokyo, Vancouver, Venice, Victoria City, Vienna and Zurich. A number of these cities we have visited more than once and there may be a few destinations I have forgotten. In our later years, we find that we enjoy cruises the most, as it is not necessary to pack and repack going from one land location to another. We have taken cruises from Vancouver through the inland passageway to Alaska, throughout the Greek Isles on several occasions, from Athens to Venice, from St. Thomas to Antigua, from St. Thomas to various ports in the Caribbean, and from Montreal to New York. We have dozens of photo albums preserving the images of all these trips and cruises. Thus two diversions, photography and travel, can be enjoyed simultaneously. Our next cruise probably will be from Costa Rico through the Panama Canal to Belize and Fort Lauderdale. At least this is a target, but at my age I don't even buy green bananas anymore.

Chapter XVI

FAMILY, FAITH, VALUES AND ETHICS

Having been raised by God-fearing and loving parents as well as grandparents in small rural Texas communities during the depression and recession years of the thirties, there could be no excuse not to have my head screwed on right when it comes to basic issues of religious faith, family values and honesty.

As I mentioned in an earlier chapter, my grandfather brought his family from South Dakota in 1909 and first located in my *hometown* of Snyder. He was one of the founders of the First Methodist Church when he first resided there and his name is on the cornerstone of its original sanctuary. He then lived in Dennison, Ranger and Tuscola before moving back to Snyder in the early forties after retiring. His philosophy was quoted in 1945 in the Snyder Daily News: "Texas is my adopted state. I love it and her people. I have tried through the years to be active in civic and church affairs; and in the declining years of my life, among old friends, my wife and I are happy in the consciousness that life has been good to us. We have traveled the road of life together for forty-eight years [fifty-seven before he passed]. I have lived from the ox-cart age to the airplane age, and am now praying that this war may soon end, and that a permanent United Nations will banish wars from the earth."

In the early 1940s he wrote a letter to his daughter, Beth, when she was having a tough time with her marriage and life, expressing his and my grandmother's profound religious beliefs. I am including it in the appendix to this book. In it, his preamble is stated simply, "To believe what fundamentally it takes to be a Christian, you only need the following brief creed: I take Jesus, the Christ, God and Son, to be my savior and I will walk in his way." I can testify to the fact that he not only talked the *talk*, he also walked the *walk* each and every day that I knew him. He did not have to prepare for death. He paid his dues as he went. When the time came, he was ill with pneumonia, and he called his family to his bedside. He sang the "Old Rugged Cross," closed his eyes and made the transition. In his letter to Beth, he described this foreseeable event: "The soul does not sleep in the grave. 'And the body shall return to the dust of the earth and the soul to God who gave it.' Christ told the dying thief: 'This day thou shalt be with me in paradise.' 'Life is continuous. The soul [the real self] never dies.'"

My parents likewise were totally committed to the same beliefs and God was always in the foreground of their rich and productive lives. My mother was always full of love and was everything anyone could ask for. She was the greeter at our church door for years before she lost life's battle to cancer. Her sister-in-law, Rose Deffebach, wrote a poem in tribute to her that says it all. It is included and preserved in the appendix to this book. I have one sister, Mary Williams, who still lives in Snyder with her husband, Tommy. They are the salt of the earth. Mary has largely followed in my mother's footsteps in giving of herself to her church. Professionally, she was a career teacher in the Snyder public schools, specializing in special education. Later in life she taught at the Price Daniel prison unit in Snyder, which one might label as a specialty in *extraspecial education.* Both teaching careers had to be challenging. She recently retired and spends her spare time helping her husband with his video business. She and Tommy have two children, Julie and Blair. Our personal relationship has strengthened in recent years and we are both happy with that. She is nine years younger; and you have to understand that while growing up in Snyder, I had to baby-sit for her when there were more exciting things to do. On the other side of the fence, she had legitimate complaints about me deviling her. For example, when we went on trips, my dad was death on rest stops unless we needed gasoline for the car. Extra stops ruined his precision schedule of the times for stops and the times we were to arrive at each and every destination. You may not understand this if you are not of German or similar descent. Knowing how extra stops brought fire and brimstone lectures by my dad, I would ask my little sister as we were riding in the backseat if she would like some chocolate candy. When she always said she would like some, I would give her several squares of Ex-lax. The results were foreseeable, and when she finally was old enough to figure it out, I can see how she might have a legitimate beef or two about her older brother. With such a kind and considerate brother, who needs any enemies?

My dad was involved in everything; the church always came first among these activities, but it didn't stop there. From 1912 to the time of his death in 1987, he was a member of the Methodist Church. He taught Sunday school classes for numerous years. He was always a member of the official board and normally a trustee of the church. He was a member and officer of the old Epworth League in the late 1920's and early 1930's. From 1960 to 1962, he was chairman of the official board of the First Methodist in Snyder. He was a board member of King's Manor Retirement Home in Hereford, the Methodist Hospital in Lubbock and the Methodist Home in Waco. He held numerous offices in the Northwest Texas Conference of the Methodist Church and was its conference Lay Leader from 1964 to 1968. He was its delegate to the National Conference in 1968-72.

He had a great love for scouting. In the mid-1930s he was a member of the Executive Board of the Chisholm Trail Council of the Boy Scouts of America. In the early 1940s he was a cub master in Snyder. From 1943 to 1983, he was a member of the executive board of the Buffalo Trail Council. He served as its president from 1953 to 1955. He was awarded the coveted Silver Beaver award by the Boy Scouts of America.

He was a Mason and a charter member of the Suez Temple Shrine. He was a member and president of the Snyder Chamber of Commerce. He was a member and president of the Snyder chapter of the International Lions Club. In the mid-1940s he was its zone chairman of Texas District 2-T-2. From 1950 to 1974, he was a member of the board of directors of the Colorado Municipal Water District, headquartered in Big Springs, Texas. He was its vice president in 1959-60. He was chairman of War Bond Sales of Scurry County for eight years. From 1955 to 1980 he served on the board of directors of the Snyder Industrial Development Corp. from 1955 to 1959, and was its president in 1957-59. In 1957, he was named Businessman of the Year by the Snyder Chamber of Commerce. In 1971, he received the Distinguished Service Award from the Rotary Club in Big Springs, recognizing his work on the Colorado River Authority which benefited the Midland—Big Springs—Snyder areas of West Texas. In 1979-83, he was a member of the board of directors of the Sears Memorial Retirement Home in Abilene, Texas.

In a nutshell, my dad didn't let much grass grow under his feet. He was a leader by example. He and my mom believed that God had blessed them in life regardless of depression, recession and war years; and they both tossed a lot back to their church, community, scouting activities and to their family and friends. My grandparents and parents were a tough act to follow. At this point in life, I do not believe I could have carried their water bucket, much less walked in their moccasins.

In my early days in El Paso, I faced a challenge when I agreed to teach an adult singles Sunday school at the Methodist Church we first attended. The first problem I encountered was that among the members of the class were the minister's daughter and a retired young Methodist minister. She was somewhat of a doubting Thomas and he had left the ministry because he felt the Methodist Church was hypocritical in its teaching. He referred to a specific instance during his ministry that I had heard my dad talk about. It took place at a general conference meeting, held in San Francisco, of the clergy and lay officers of the various conferences around the country several years before. The first item on the conference agenda was to affirm the church's historical position on total abstinence from alcohol. The referendum was overwhelmingly passed. The second agenda item also dealt with alcohol, but in the context of restrictive clauses which the church used in deeding property which was no longer needed for church purposes. It had always required a prohibition in its deeds banning the future use of alcohol forever on the property sold. That year, there was considerable debate as to the use of such a covenant and its economic effect on the market value of the property sold. The church conference reversed it previous stand on the issue and overwhelmingly passed a referendum that would allow its property to be sold with no prohibition on the future use of alcohol on it. It was coincidental that my dad was the conference lay leader for the Northwest Texas Conference that year and was the conference's delegate to this meeting that the young minister from El Paso had reference to when telling others why he left the ministry.

In any event, the local minister's daughter and the ex-minister made my preparation for the class tough and they both loved to test my religion in every possible way. The bottom line was that I knew the parts of the Bible we studied during this period much better than anytime in the past, even when as a kid we read the Bible from cover to cover on two different occasions. I managed to survive this class by developing class participation from all class members other than these two, in order to create more balance. I had to learn to have a flexible lesson plan each Sunday. In a way, it is like trying a law case. If you have the law in your favor in a particular case, hammer on the law; if you have the facts but not the law on your side, argue the equities flowing from the facts; and if you do not have the law or the facts on your side, just pound on the counsel table to divert the jury. A corollary to this saying that relates to teaching an adult singles' Sunday school class would be that if you have five percent of the class that are troublemakers, call on the other nine-five percent of the class regularly to recite and give their views on the subject matter at hand. At least, this reduces the teacher beating some of the time. Of course, I am kidding, as I have to credit the two problem members with improving both my Bible and speaking skills during the two years I taught the class. Later, we moved our church home and joined Western Hills Methodist Church, which was on the west side of the mountains in El Paso and nearer home. Until leaving El Paso to move to Houston, I was a member of its administrative board and its board of trustees.

I remained a Methodist until my conversion to Catholicism in the early 1990s. This occurred after we met through Catholic friends Archbishop Oscar Lipscomb of Mobile, Alabama. We traveled extensively with him and our friends, Raye and Ed White. The archbishop is a cousin of Ed White. After three audiences with Pope John Paul II as a Methodist and with my wife as an Episcopalian, we found a religion that fit both of us and our beliefs. We already had rosaries, which the pope had given us when he invited us to early morning mass at Castel Gandolfo, his summer residence. These rosaries are treasured gifts as there is no source for ones with the papal seal but the pope. To put it in context, Luciano Pavaritti, the famed Italian tenor, in the book "Art of Giving," describes this gift from the pope as his greatest treasure. We were confirmed several years later after studying Catholicism for about a year and completing the required documentation under Canon Law. The mass was celebrated by Archbishop Lipscomb with our local priest, Father Joseph Doyle, as concelebrants. We owe a lot to Archbishop Lipscomb who has had a considerable influence in our lives. In addition, he introduced us in Rome to Bishop Curtis Guillory, who was one of the auxiliary bishops in our Houston-Galveston Diocese. Later, he was appointed by the pope to serve as the bishop of the Beaumont Diocese. He has become a really close personal friend and is a great source of inspiration and spiritual guidance. Father Doyle also played an important part in our lives and has now been transferred by his order to Tampa, Florida, to serve as President of Jesuit High School.

In 1999, my wife and I were elected by the *Vatican* as a *lady* and *knight* of *The Equestrian Order of the Holy Sepulchre of Jerusalem*. Our nomination was by Bishop Fiorenza of the Galveston-Houston Diocese. The Order is the only one under the protection of the Holy See, and membership is considered one of the highest papal awards conferred upon clergy and laity alike. Pope John Paul II describes it this way: "May the honor that comes to you through membership in our Equestrian Order make you feel more and more the burden and responsibility of distinguishing your toil with an exemplary Christian life and with consistent generous and disinterested adherence to Christ and to the Church. In this way, you will give before the world the best confirmation of the reason for its existence and activity."

I recently went to a Christian breakfast for the greater Houston area. It's an annual event and thanks to our doctor and friend, Philip C. Johnson III, I was also invited and attended last year's breakfast. The program and speakers were excellent on both occasions. They were also very patriotic—opening with a prayer, Bible readings, the pledge to the flag and the singing of the national anthem. Yes, we pledged allegiance to our flag and nation, *under God!* This year's speaker was Charlie Duke, the former NASA astronaut who served as the lunar module pilot of *Apollo 16*. He and John Young were on this first scientific expedition to the moon to inspect, survey and sample materials in the rugged lunar highlands. They logged more than seventy-one hours on the mission. Counting three subsequent lunar stays, they logged more than twenty hours in *Rover 2* over the roughest surface yet encountered on the moon.

Charlie spoke of his career and his personal life. First, he teed up his presentation by noting the reference to a nation *under God* in the pledge to our flag. Upon his retirement from NASA in 1975, he asked himself if his life was *under* God. His response and the rest of his talk described a lot of people I know, including myself at the time I retired. God was always there, out there *somewhere*; and Charlie says that he had gone to church almost every Sunday as a good Christian should. But that was it. The simple fact was Charlie found that God was not first in his heart. Instead, he was full of himself and his amazing career. He had graduated as valedictorian from Admiral Farragut Academy in St. Petersburg, Florida. He had earned his BS degree from the U.S. Naval Academy and his MS degree from the Massachusetts Institute of Technology. Since the air force did not then have an academy, he volunteered to receive his commission in the air force, entered pilot training, earned his wings in 1958 and served three years as a fighter interceptor. He was selected in the Apollo program in 1966. When he retired in 1975 from NASA, he entered the air force reserves, achieving the rank of brigadier general before retiring from the air force in 1986.

As of this writing, only twenty-four persons have walked on the moon. In his self-analysis, Charlie says he didn't do any of this for fame or fortune. He illustrates this by saying that he has yet to sit down beside someone on a commercial airplane flight, for example, and have them say, "Hey, aren't you Charlie Duke, the astronaut that spend so much time on the moon?" As for the money, Charlie reminded us that he only received a lieutenant colonel's pay while going back and forth to the moon. He joking said that he couldn't get NASA to pay him a mileage allowance of five cents a mile for space travel. This would have helped financially, since each one-way trip is about 260,000 miles.

Charlie was able to borrow $1.5 million to start a business, which he stated had also been successful. But with all this success, he was not fulfilled. He felt his marriage was in trouble. About the time he was thinking about his situation and the fact that God was not first in his heart, he somewhat reluctantly accepted an invitation to attend a weekend retreat for Bible study. At the retreat, he came into contact with those who helped him find the answer. He said that it caused him to realize that his career, adventure and money were all that had been in his heart. This is true of so many people as they pursue *success* in life, and normally if they finally achieve financial independence, it is sometimes too late to learn that wealth and material things do not create happiness. Charlie started to change his life immediately. The first thing he did was to apologize to his wife and ask her for forgiveness. Then he did the same with his young sons; although he had spent time with them, it was more in the role of a drill sergeant. He was quick to explode verbally at them and others and find fault with most everything they did. It is hard for a perfectionist to accept less from others, especially his family and business associates.

Now, Charlie is *under* God in the sense God is *first* in his heart followed closely by his wife and family. At this point, he asked that his wife, who was in the audience at the prayer breakfast of over one thousand people, to stand and be acknowledged. He thanked her for forgiving him for putting his own success in front of God and family. Since his spiritual awakening, he told the audience that he has found contentment and happiness. This was a great testimonial and I saw many a handkerchief go to the eye during Charlie's talk. This wonderful testimonial was heard by a group of Christians assembled for the specific purpose of a prayer breakfast. Oh, how I wish his message could be heard by agnostics and nonbelievers as well.

When my business partner, Fred Schneider, and I sold our Houston automobile dealerships to Roger Penske, I had some cash to put away for retirement. I, like Charlie, also realized that I had not reached a point of contentment and inner peace. Somewhat like Charlie, I started attending a regular weekly Bible study group. My wife and our doctor had conspired to bring this about. As noted earlier, Phil Johnson is the family doctor and one of the best Christian lay persons I ever met. There are huge demands on his time at work and elsewhere. Yet he is a major player in his church, Pines Presbyterian Church, located in west Houston. He attends several Bible study groups, but I started attending one with him that meets at 7 AM on Tuesday mornings. Normally, except when out of town for vacation or the like, the class is led by the pastor of the church, Wayne Eberly. He has been at the church for about ten years and still looks like a schoolboy. He is dynamic and has a great deal of charisma. I refer to him as our young and fearless leader. He is fearless because he has to manage our group with an average age of about seventy-one. There was an incident that took place before my time when an older member of the group took issue with something Wayne had said and the older member walked out of the session bitter and angry. Wayne worked with him thereafter, and finally convinced him to attend private sessions in Wayne's office each week to talk about the Bible in general and to read and discuss scriptures together. The pastor finally won him over and he returned to the Tuesday morning group. He contributed regularly to our discussions after I joined the group, until he recently died. Our group attended the funeral and sat together. At the request of the family, Wayne did the funeral and handled it in such a way that everyone was touched. Our young and fearless leader had worked hard, did not give up and, at the close of the day had made a friend out of someone who could have been a cloud over his ministry

When Wayne cannot attend, the group is led by one of the group. We average about thirty five or so attendees each week. Maybe two of them are in their thirties, Wayne is in his early forties, Phil is in his fifties and the rest are much older with the senior member, Al Kaeppel, being ninety-seven years young. I am including in this book a photograph of the group celebrating his birthday. About the only noticeable problem in the class is that we have a rather high attrition rate. In the past twelve months, we had five members pass. But it is a joy to discuss the Bible and current events with this group. Most are retired, but their work backgrounds are quite varied and significant. Several hold or are responsible for patented inventions. One is a member of the distinguished *Texas Business Hall of Fame.* I was privileged to attend one of their early functions when Sam Young was so honored. Quite a few have major corporate experience with companies such as Exxon, Shell and the like. All are real gentlemen and bring something to the table regularly. I am the only remaining *token* Catholic in the group as we recently lost our friend, Lamar Seegars, who was also Catholic. There are members of this group who are from other religious faiths and/or other Presbyterian churches in Houston.

This has been a very rewarding experience for me, and I am trying to make the most of this wonderful opportunity that came my way. Almost without exception, the members actually look forward to arising at the crack of dawn, or before depending on the time of the year, to come to the group sessions. Few are willing to miss a weekly session unless they are out of town, ill, disabled, hospitalized or have work or other meaningful conflicts. It says a lot for the value and quality of the study and discussions which occur each week. One member of the class, Tom Potts, has written the memoirs of his life during the twentieth century, entitled *Chilton Street.* Tom has given me meaningful pointers relative to this book, and I am indebted to him for his help and advice. Jim Anderson volunteered technical assistance which was invaluable. Jim is active in the business information service business and devotes a lot of time to the church in fine-tuning its sound systems. The group has done a lot to move me in the direction of putting God *first* in my heart, closely followed by the love of my wife, Carolyn, our children, other family and friends. I still have work to do and lots to learn, but I am now on the path I will travel from this point forward.

As noted previously, I have been married twice. As a result, I have learned over the years that it is important to marry for the right reasons. I married the first time as I was graduating from college, as that was the thing most everyone did and it was expected by my parents and peers. Before I was married the second time, I had learned that I had not been ready for marriage at age twenty-one. Generally speaking, women mature sooner than men. I didn't really mature until the USMC humbled me. Then I realized that I was not as smart as I had thought in my late teens and early twenties. When I was separated from active duty with the marines, I had then come to realize that my parents were the smart ones, which was not always my vision during my teen years.

By the time I married the second time, I had developed the belief that a successful marriage must be a two-way street and its Rx to last requires *(1) a commitment between best friends, (2) an economic and spiritual partnership bottomed upon a belief in God and family values, (3) a sharing and caring relationship for each other* and *(4) each partner must have a willingness to communicate about problem areas and to compromise to resolve issues.* A new friend of mine, Elliot Gershenson, president and CEO of the Interfaith Ministries of Greater Houston wrote a great letter about marriage to both his son and daughter when each was engaged. He told them that this was his first *real* gift to them, and he hoped that they and their respective spouses would take the time to read it carefully and to reread it at times when they might need a lift and renewed strength as they encountered obstacles to hurdle during marriage. The letter, *inter alia*, contained the following advice which expands beautifully on my shorthand rendition of the prescription above for a successful marriage:

"First and foremost, remember that you are each other's *best friend*. Friends understand each other. They share an ultimate trust. They are not easily disappointed in one another—for they know that no one is perfect. They give each other space to be separate beings, while depending on each other to be there. They are also willing to compromise for the sake of their *commitment to each other*.

"Don't be afraid to be angry with one another. *Sharing* how you feel, even at the most trying times, is the true test of a loving and deep relationship. It is easy to tell your *partner* things he or she wants to hear. It is equally important to share difficult thoughts—so you feel fully understood. You do not have to agree—you only have to agree that you will work things out.

"Don't stop talking to each other, no matter what. Holding things inside, especially angry feelings, leads to isolation and discord. *Pledge to resolve your issues*, even when they are heated.

"Neither *partner* is the senior partner. There will be areas of your home life where one of you takes the lead. There will be others where you share more or less equally. The better you identify each area, the less likely that you will feel dissonance in your relationship. Ultimately, a real *equal partnership* makes for the greatest team. And marriage is a team effort.

"A *God-centered home* provides a basis for thankfulness. When you believe that there is something more fundamental than your own needs, you can then focus on the needs of others—those of your spouse, those of your children. All you really need to know is that God has made you both in His image, and you can be thankful that He made it possible for you to have each other—in both good and bad times. If you cannot see God in this way, then all the rituals and laws have little meaning to your earthly lives.

"Don't take life too seriously, but be serious about your life. You will have many ups and downs together. It is these episodes which will make the story of your life so special. Strive to be better each day, while accepting each other's limitations.

"And finally, *share a vision* for your future. Articulate it so often that it no longer needs to be said. Know in your heart that you both stand for the same overall principles, that you *share the same* goals and aspirations. Don't get too far ahead of one another, so that your inevitable changes mirror one another. Let your individually shine, but not at the expense of your shared life."

Elliot also told his kids to keep a Jewish home. "It is like an anchor in a world that is too often adrift in a mindless sea." He also reminds them that marriage is hard work and not to be fooled by the early spark of love. "If you are to succeed, it will be because you always will remember what it is that drew you together in the first place, and decided to build on the true spark of *trust, love, compromise, commitment, faithfulness and honesty.*"

Where emphasis has been added to the quotes from Elliot's letter, it is that of this author, for the purpose of reflecting the similarities in our thinking about the nuts and bolts of what it takes to have a lasting marriage. I appreciate Elliot's consent to quote extensively from his wonderful *gift* to his children and their intended spouses.

There is another potential problem that many families encounter other than making their marriage last. It concerns how to maintain a close and meaningful relationship with all your children. This subject has caused difficulty for me and many a sleepless night. I have three natural children, two sons and a daughter. The daughter, Susan, is the oldest, married with no children and lives in California. It has been a number of years since we have communicated or spoken. Her first husband was my partner's son. They split in such a way that my partner could never forgive her for divorcing his son. I am sure that there was enough blame to go around, but my partner cannot overlook that she then remarried one of our company's employees. We all had grief with the divorce and her subsequent remarriage; however, a number of years later she and her husband returned for a time to Houston and my wife and I were able to put some of the pieces together as far as our relationship was concerned. Then she and her husband left Houston and moved elsewhere. We still were able to communicate from time to time by telephone. She was then working for a vendor supplying services to one of the car importers for which we had a franchise to sell its products.

At one of the importer's annual car shows, my daughter encountered my partner, each in the company of one of the importer's employees. There was some type of acknowledgement of each other and they walked away. The person with my partner asked him how he knew Susan. He made some comment on the divorce with his son and the fact she had remarried one of our former employees. Apparently, the comment after passing through several of the importer employees' mouths got back to my daughter. She must have called her husband who had not attended the show and he called me that night. His speech was somewhat slurred, but I got the gist of what she had told him happened. He asked me if it would do any good for him to call my partner and explain how much time had expired since the divorce, and then tell him that it was time to drop all the old hard feelings. That is all that he asked me. I told him that it was my opinion, knowing the depth of my partner's feeling over the matter, it would probably not do any good for him to call my partner because he had not changed his opinion of the matter since it happened. My son-in-law seemed to agree with that conclusion.

After I hung up talking to him, I placed a call for my daughter to discuss the matter with her. She was not at home, but I left a message on the answering machine asking her to call me at her earliest convenience. She never did and I am clueless as to why not. I have no idea if her husband told her that the only thing he asked me that night was whether I thought it would do any good for him to call my partner. As he sounded somewhat confused, he may not have accurately relayed our conversation to her. In any event, I have never heard from her since. I talked to my partner the day he returned from the car show, and he confirmed what generally he had told the importer's employee with him. He also apologized for whatever hurt it caused me but reiterated that he still could not forgive her for what she had done to his son.

I am also *sans* communication with my eldest son, Lyle, who was named for my father, but at least I understand what the problem is with him. We always had a good relationship and communicated often, even though he lived and worked in another city after college. At some point of time, we realized that it had been some time since we had heard from him. We knew he had moved to another area near the same city, but he had not given us his telephone number. While trying to secure his new number and address, we stumbled on two facts I did not know. He had secured a legal name change so that he had abandoned the family surname and now used his middle given name as his new surname. Secondly, he had married a lady and had a ready-made family with two stepdaughters. My wife made a number of attempts to reach him and finally succeeded. He had seemed reluctant to discuss either his new family or the name change. After several more calls by us to him, he agreed to bring his family to Houston to visit. Everything seemed to be all right, and we had a good visit and later several more, including his participation in our youngest son's wedding. During their last visit, my wife finally asked him why on earth he had changed his name. His wife blew sky high and wouldn't let him answer. Finally, she blurted out that she was the one who had asked him to change his last name because she couldn't pronounce it; so how could she expect her teenage daughters to pronounce it? She summoned our son out of the room and they went upstairs without another word being said. We had friends coming over and all of us were going out to dinner that evening.

Just before they arrived, our daughter-in-law knocked on the bathroom door as we were dressing. When I told her we would be out in a minute and we were not dressed, she just marched in anyway and told us she was leaving with her family, as she was uncomfortable in our home and having us quiz Lyle about the name change. We asked him to discuss the matter with us, as he had not said a word the whole time. She instructed him not to talk to us and to leave the house immediately. It was obviously planned since their luggage was at the front door. Out they marched as our friends were arriving at the front door. They tried to greet them, but were blown out by the exodus. Once again, we have not heard a word from them but it is abundantly clear who wears the pants in their house.

It is difficult for me to understand the iron curtain of silence from my two oldest children. I could never have built a wall between myself and my parents no matter what. I realize that there are also some issues relative to my second marriage, but these had been put aside before the melt down in both cases. It is not my place to judge their actions. I think there is some miscommunication involved in what my daughter's husband told her about his call to me and my response. I do not know that for a fact, but I do know what he asked me and what I told him. I know that my son's wife was dominant enough to cause him to change his surname. If I were he, I would have been proud to be named for my father and his grandfather, and there is no way I could have considered changing my surname. Not even if my wife, whom I love dearly, had made it a condition of marriage. Of course, she is as upset as I am over the name change. I witnessed his domination when his wife marched him out of our home in front of family friends and refused to let him talk to us. I pray that he knows how much we love him and regret what happened. I wish both of these children the best in life and hope that someday, someway the problems can be overcome. In the meantime, I accept the fact that every story has two sides, and I accept any blame that may be laid at my doorstep. The bottom line is that I consider the situation a major disappointment in my life and a failure somewhere along the line in my parenting skills.

Conversely, our youngest son, Matthew, is a parent's reward. We also love our new daughter, Kathy, who he married on May 25, 2002. He is practicing law in Houston with a major firm, and she held a responsible position in the regional Multiple Dystrophy office located in Houston until recently. While there, she was quite busy with MD administration, the firemen's boot and like fund raising activities as well as the annual Jerry Lewis Telethon partnered in Houston by Channel 2. She resigned a week or so ago because she and Matt would like to start their family with Kathy as a stay-at-home mom [the good Lord willing].

Brett was my wife's youngest son by a prior marriage and I adopted him. After he graduated from college, we had some problems with some of his choices. Gradually, we worked these differences out to the point that we now have regular contact with him. He has spent a number of years in California working on psychology degrees and licensing. He will probably soon relocate to establish a practice somewhere other than Los Angeles. We enjoy our friendly, and sometimes lengthy, telephone conversations with him. Normally, he also makes about one trip a year to Houston to visit and also to see old friends. It's a pleasure to know that distance alone does not separate children and parents.

Our extended family also includes our good and faithful housekeeper, Maria Requena, who has been with us for many years. She has also been a loving and invaluable care giver for my wife in recent years. Last but not least, Maria has made sure that the youngest member of our family, *Little Bit*, a seven pound Bichon Frise, is bilingual.

I would like to pass on an idea that I first heard of when waiting in Phil Johnson's office for my wife's appointment. The reading material in his office is mostly about family health and values. The magazine I picked up to kill time contained an article about ethical wills. I practiced law actively for nearly twenty years and have been licensed to do so by the State of Texas for almost fifty years. I had never heard of an ethical will. I read the article with great interest. It is not a complicated subject. We all know about last wills and testaments by which we leave our *worldly things* to our family and others. But the author of this article was saying that we should leave some type of written document behind for those who come after us to remember and understand what *values* we stood for and what *lessons of life* we wanted to pass on to them. For example, I think my grandfather's letter to his daughter [located in the appendix] qualifies as an *ethical will.* Taking the concept one step further, I prepared a Bible study presentation on it for the group at Pines Presbyterian Church. In developing the subject matter, it also occurred to me that this is really why we have a Holy Bible. I believe the writers of the various books of the Bible wanted to document the experiences, beliefs and interpretations of not only themselves but also of others for the benefit and guidance of future generations, in order that those that followed them would not be dependent on only word-of-mouth renditions. To me, it makes good sense because we all know what can happen by telling someone of an experience, event or even gossip, and then having it come back to you from another source six times removed in a form that you can hardly recognize the story you put into motion. The shorthand answer is, of course, that the people who hear a story usually embellish it to some degree in passing it on to others. Thus, it can change in meaning and emphasis in many cases.

This concept was largely the motivation for writing this book. It is principally for my descendants who come after me. I wanted to define the roots of my family's origination in Germany to the present time in some more permanent and condensed version that the some nine hundred pages of family history contained in the booklets that I have prepared over the last several years, containing the research efforts of myself and our family members, particularly those of Sharon R. Deffebach, Randy Baxter and Will, Daryl and Elden Deffenbaugh. It is difficult to imagine that this genealogy project originated with a one page family tree of some of our ancestors drawn by my dad in ink that I found in his personal effects after his death.

In this chapter, I have touched on the most significant areas of my family background, my parents' dedication to family values and the significance of putting God first in your heart. I want to close by mentioning a few of life's lessons, ethical and otherwise, that might be contained in my last will and testament of *values and other intangible thoughts*, as opposed to the one that I leave disposing of *things*. Just as *things* are not necessarily invented by their owners, some of these *thoughts* are not necessarily original to me, but rather are impressions arising from *seeds* implanted in my mind from numerous sources, encounters and contacts during my lifetime. I have assembled, organized and classified them in my mind as worthwhile goals or learning experiences that I want to pass on to those who follow me.

In life's endeavors, one must *lead, follow or step aside.* No one has the market cornered on how to develop leadership abilities. There are, however, a number of talents, personality traits and circumstances required to assume a leadership position. For starters, I would suggest that anyone seeking leadership responsibility consider what I call the *Ten Commandments of Leadership:*

Rule One: The opportunity to lead must come your way, but always be alert so you can contribute to the creation of an opportunity.

Rule Two: A leader must care for the people led and be sensitive to their needs in order to earn their respect.

Rule Three: For most, it takes a measure of ego to create the desire to lead, and a leader has to enjoy competition and be driven by the need to do his or her best at all times. But ego should only bring you to the door of the opportunity to lead and should never be permitted to override the other commandments for quality leadership.

Rule Four: A good leader must be knowledgeable about the subject matter requiring leadership. For example, a good sales manager cannot effectively lead salespersons unless he or she possesses superior product knowledge and understands what makes the potential customer tick.

Rule Five: A leader must have some tolerance for risk taking and must always learn from his or her mistakes as well as successes. Good judgment often comes from a bad experience, which often happens due to bad judgment.

Rule Six: Never abandon common sense for love of self or any other reason, and a leader must have enough common sense to improvise when the need arises. There are simply times when a leader has to think out of the box or at least push the envelope to develop reasonable solutions to problems and to accomplish goals.

Rule Seven: An effective leader never mentally leaves his or her receiver off the hook, as he or she must be a good listener. Said another way, you never learn anything when it's your mouth that is moving.

Rule Eight: Do not ask anyone under your leadership to do anything you are not willing to do yourself.

Rule Nine: Praise your followers in public, and censure only in private; otherwise, you have conclusively demonstrated you do not understand this short course in Leadership 101 as you have violated Rules Two and Six.

Rule Ten: Finally, if your leadership abilities carry you to the top in a business or profession, continue to handle problems promptly. They always get worse with age. Do not procrastinate or ignore them because that does not lessen the problem nor alter the facts that give rise to it. The buck should always stop at your desk, and one should not forget that *companies, like trees, die from the top down.*

Recognize, of course, that not everyone is cut out for a leadership role in life. There are naturally more *followers* than *leaders*, just as there were more Indians than chiefs. There is absolutely nothing wrong in being a follower; and many are the salt of the earth. A *good* follower is one who can (1) be loyal and honest to their leader, (2) learn to be happy with his or her work or assignment and (3) give a full measure of value in return for his or her pay. If you are unable to qualify under these guidelines, it is time to change leaders or jobs. What is really important is not to be a *step aside*, just sitting on the sidelines letting others provide for you as life passes you by. If you play this card, you will never have any sense of pride nor develop self esteem.

Do not confuse the *power to lead* with the actual exercise of good leadership skills enumerated in the *Ten Commandments* above, and do not become obsessed with *power* alone as it is not absolute. Its flip side is *responsibility*. An extreme example can be illustrated by the time I took my turn as one of the two marines who anchored the rope for the climb to the roof of a seven-story building. I had the *power* to let go of the rope at any time and cause grievous injury or death to the marine on his way up; but because of the awesome *responsibility* I felt as a consequence of that *power*, there is no way that I was going to let that marine down even if he had been my worst enemy.

Other lessons I have learned or observed during my bountiful life and would like to give and bequeath to those who follow me are:

Lesson 1: You will go far if you adopt a philosophy that everyone you come in contact with should be *greeted with a smile and a kind word*. It costs little but will usually mean a lot to the recipient. Some where along life's path, you will probably receive a great return on this investment, because under everyone's hard façade is the spirit of a person who wants to be appreciated. Often it is the *small things* we do that makes life worth living.

Lesson 2: Always attempt to speak *softly and tenderly*. There is also a likely return on this lesson because often we have to eat our words.

Lesson 3: Even if there is no specific law or rule that prohibits it, do not do anything or omit doing something that doesn't pass the *smell test*. This, of course, is tested by your *conscience*, not your *nose*.

Lesson 4: God did not do it all in one day, so remember that neither can you. As a general rule, I have found over the years that the *less time* I have to do work, the *more* I get done.

Lesson 5: Money does not buy *happiness or class*. Those items simply cannot be bought. Most of us desire to achieve and get to *the top*, whatever that might mean to any given person. But real growth, achievement, self-satisfaction and happiness are more likely to exist by making the *most* of every opportunity that comes your way as you struggle up the ladder to whatever you envision to be *the top*.

Lesson 6: *God will provide*, but not *too much*. The truly wise are thankful that God does not give us everything we ask for.

Lesson 7: Lastly but in no way the least important, do not confuse *someday* or *tomorrow* with *today*, or you may miss the boat. Today is the *present* and it is a gift from God. Tomorrow and someday are *mysteries*, and no one has the power to make either happen. Accordingly, use *today* wisely! For example, who among us would not have liked to have had *one more chance* to have told their mom, dad, spouse or other loved one how much we loved and cared for them before they passed away?

The fat lady has now sung, the opera is over and my tale has been told. Thanks for reading it!

APPENDIX

PHOTO ALBUM

ROOTS

Plaza in Weisloch, Germany

John Adam Deffebach Family. Seated from left: Elizabeth (holding Anna), John Adam (holding Harriet) and Charles. Standing from left: Thomas George and Arthur

Thomas George Deffebach Family. Seated on floor: Mary Ellen, Don. Seated from left: Mary Ethlyn, Florence Elizabeth, Thomas George, Ethlyn, Vernon, Annabeth. Standing from left: George Ownby, Edwina, Arthur, Lyle, Franc Irene, Bill, Nell, Thomas Melvin and Rose

Son Matt on John's Avenue, Moriah Cemetery,
Deadwood, South Dakota

John Adam's restored tombstone

John Adam's original tombstone

Tombstone of Will Bill Hickok

Tombstone of Calamity Jane

AUTHOR'S EARLY DAYS

Jimmy, the goat, and friends

Winters kids, including first girlfriend, Ira June; I am second from the right with the diamond patch on my overalls

Fishing on the Llano River

Our first home in Snyder

Mom with Uncle Arthur relaxing on the porch

LAW SCHOOL

Dean Page Keeton in Assault and Flattery

Author receiving *Senior with the Most Promise of Achieving Distinction* award

Author receiving *Phi Delta Phi Graduate of the Year* award

Law Day recognition of *Chancellors*, I am second from left

AUTOMOBILE DEALER

Goodson Honda North

Goodson Honda West

Fred's mother, Mary, *Chairman of the Board*

Fred and Bill Fishing

Mr. Honda serving wine to my wife, after swapping jackets with a waiter

The Hondas and the Deffebachs

Honda National Dealer Council, I am fifth from the left

National Loan Bank Certificate

GOLFERS

CBS Golf Commentator David Feherty and Author

CBS Sports Autographed Banner

Hey, this one actually stayed on the green

Mr. President, do you really think your son wants your job?

Kenny Perry

Lee Janzen

Curtis Strange

Fred Couples

Chris Riley

Fuzzy Zoeller

Craig Stadler

Gary McCord

Corey Pavin

Steve Pate

Jeff Shuman

Brad Faxon

Roger Maltie

Larry Mize

1992 Honda Classic with playing partners from left to right: "Willie," a vice president of Honda; the Weston Hills golf course developer; Steve Pate, the defending champion; Dan Marino, Miami Dolphin quarterback; and one player in stars and stripes who will remain nameless due to slicing his first drive into the food tent with hundreds of Marino's *groupies* watching

TRAVELS

Bill and Carolyn in Hawaii

Carolyn on Seven Mile Beach, Grand Cayman

Carolyn eating in Oslo

Local boats escorting the cruise ship Norway on its maiden voyage to Oslo

Ephesus Archway

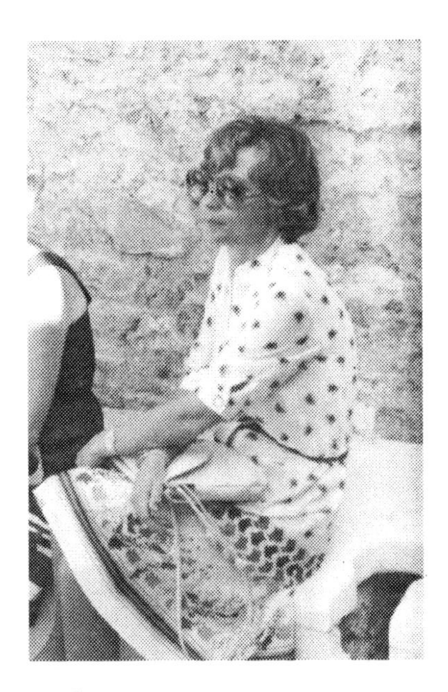

Carolyn resting in ancient 24 "holer" in Ephesus

Carolyn and Bill in Venice

Raye White, Archbishop Lipscomb, Carolyn and myself posing at the entrance of the Red Dog Saloon in Skagway

Carolyn in Hong Kong with daughter of Chinese friends

Carolyn and Bill in Hyde Park, London

Ed White, myself and Dr. Leslie Dornfeld in Acapulco

Carolyn, Myself, Monsignor Ollie Adams, Raye White, Archbishop Lipscomb, Grazi Dornfeld and Dr. Leslie Dornfeld in Acapulco

Raye White, Carolyn, Archbishop Lipscomb and Ed White in Florence, Italy

Archbishop Lipscomb celebrating mass in Assisi

Spanish steps in Rome

Taos, New Mexico

United States Military Academy viewed from the Hudson River on a cruise from Montreal to New York City

RELIGIOUS

Castel Gandolfo, summer residence of the pope

Swiss guards at the entrance

Pope John Paul II with Archbishop Lipscomb
celebrating mass in the garden of Castel Gandolfo

The Pope presents Carolyn with a papal rosary

The Pope arrives in the pope-mobile in St. Peter's Square

The Pope at the alter

Carolyn, Bill, Archbishop Lipscomb and Pope John Paul II

Archbishop Lipscomb celebrating mass in our home

Bishop Curtis Guillory,
Bishop of the Beaumont Diocese in Beaumont, Texas

St. Joseph Catholic Parish, our church home in Houston

Father Joseph Doyle, the priest of St. Joseph Parish at the time of our confirmation and who is now president of Jesuit High School, Tampa, Florida

The men's Tuesday morning Bible study group at Pines Presbyterian Church, celebrating Al Kaeppel's ninety seventh birthday

Al's response several days later; he was the in-house artist for the Humble Oil & Refining Company (now Exxon)

FAMILY & FRIENDS

My mom

My dad

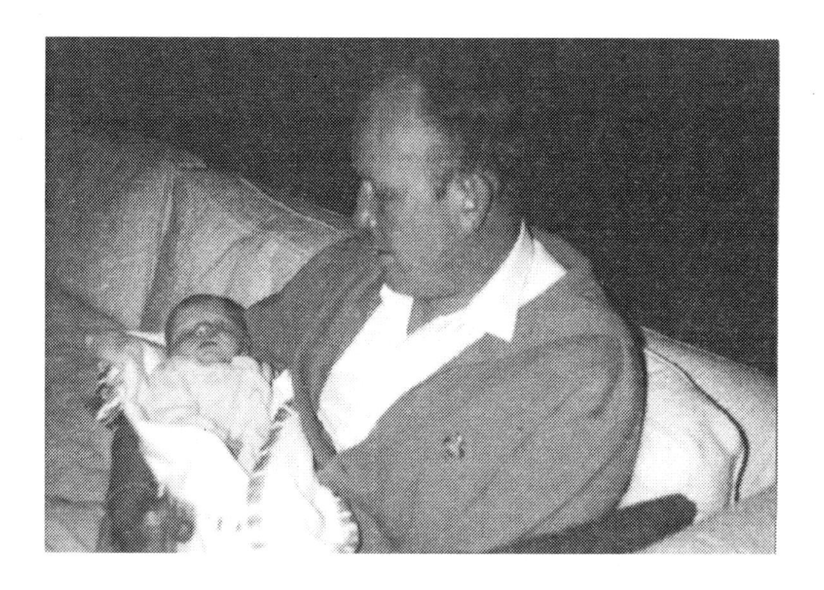

Holding Matt as an infant

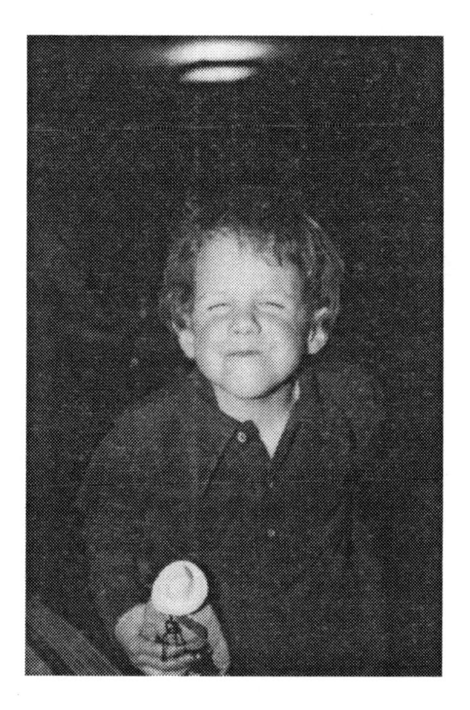

Young Matt with red hair

Kathy and Matt leaving the altar as wife and husband

Kathy and Matt leaving the church, but couldn't wait

Kathy and Matt at the reception

Kathy and Carolyn

Matt dancing with his mom

Mom and Brett

Fred Schneider with his wife, Susan, and grandson, Fred

Anita and David Feherty

Godson Fred, Bill, Carolyn, Goddaughter Erin and Willie

Bill, Erin, Carolyn and Fred

Fred, Bill and Karl

Anita and Erin

Karl and Anita

Willie, Erin and Karl

Erin

Linda and Dr. Phil Johnson

Liz and Greg McCormick

Janice, Larry and Robert Finder

Irene and Jack Townsend

Janet and Bruce Flohr

Young Fred K. Schneider Jr.

Young Karl Schneider

The eagle scout badge is one used today; the badge below is my original badge in sterling silver issued June 18, 1946

Maria Requena, our beloved housekeeper and caregiver, with *Little Bit*, our seven pound Bichon Frise

An Approach to the Study of Law

By: Bill Deffebach, Teaching Quizmaster

Undoubtedly, one of the first rumors to greet the entering first-year student concerns the high percentage of failures to be expected among his or her class. As compared to their previous educational endeavors, it is generally true that a substantial number of their law classmates will not succeed. But it is nonsense to speak of failures in terms of fixed percentages. Success or failure in law school is an individual matter. If one is mentally and emotionally equipped for the study of law and knows how to use his or her mind to the best advantage, the student will succeed.

The 'if' of course is a big one. Although it is not the purpose of this paper to state "the" solution for the removal of that condition, it will present the essentials of the learning process, related to the study of law, with which the individual student may tailor "a" solution according to the student's own needs. At least, it should be pointed out to many students that they have not yet really learned to study.

I. The Tools of the Student

The first step toward becoming a good student of the law is to acquire the necessary casebooks, notebooks and other writing materials. Questions concerning the various types of notebooks arise frequently from new students. Basically, most students employ one of three types:

(1) A spiral notebook with lined sheets and broad or narrow margins,
(2) A hardback notebook,
(3) A regular loose-leaf notebook.

The varying uses to which each is put will be discussed in a subsequent paragraph, but the student's choice of materials should depend generally upon his or her own convenience and personal preference. The first two types are advantageous because they are in permanent form for possible postlaw school reference. Flexibility is best achieved by employing the third type, but the first type, to a lesser extent, also possesses this desirable characteristic.

Most accredited law schools employ the case method of instruction, as opposed to the much—older text system. This is true of our law school. Therefore, the casebook is the chief tool of the law student. If it is economically feasible, the student should acquire the assigned casebook for each of his or her courses. Some students try to get by without a full set, hoping to borrow from friends or using the library copies when possible. Theoretically, this is possible but, as a practical matter, it is seldom satisfactory. Unfortunately, the new law student cannot afford to get behind in assignments, and frequently borrowed books will not always be available when needed. Thus, it would seem that scrimping on casebooks is false economy. Compared with the time and money that students invest in their professional training, the cost of casebooks is not excessive. Except to the extent that used casebooks can be utilized, save elsewhere! And remember further that many of these books will become old friends during the course of events and you may want to retain them for later reference or guidance in actual practice. Many of your professors will undoubtedly stress this latter point in the classroom.

One of the greatest problems facing the new student is that of learning to speak the same language as the professor.

Effective communication between the two is impossible until this has been accomplished. The process is unfortunately slow, and often it is well into the second semester before this problem is completely solved. Since the matter of legal terminology is so important to the learning process, it is not surprising that nearly all students possess a good law dictionary. These are available at the local bookstores and are, indeed, a wise investment. Although the law dictionary is not a complete solution to the communication problem, its use in conjunction with daily reading assignments is a good start as well as a practical necessity.

There are often several textbooks available to supplement any given law school course. Many new students find themselves in a quandary as to how many, if any, of these textbooks (often called "hornbooks") to purchase. Most would agree that the vast majority of these books are a definite aid in the pursuit of legal knowledge. But most are expensive. Moreover, they are time consuming, and your casebook and class notes should not be slighted in this respect. Thus, expense and time are the limiting factors regarding the purchase of textbooks. It should also be remembered that the library has a number of copies of many of these books, and the number of students desiring to use them is not necessarily prohibitive.

The new student frequently requests advice on the desirability of using "canned" briefs and outlines. These so-called study aids are generally not worthwhile from either the standpoint of time or expense. They are often distributed on a national basis without regard to the emphasis placed on a particular case or topic by the local professor. Further, one should not rely heavily on material prepared by those who can find no better use for their legal talents. Occasionally, one might find an outline prepared by local students that would be reliable and helpful. However, no outline or brief prepared by another should take the place of one that you have prepared.

The course in legal bibliography will expose you to numerous books available in the library. Because the course is time consuming, many new students tend to take it lightly. This is unquestionably a mistake! It is a bread-and-butter course, and in many respects the most important single course in the law school curriculum. Do not sell this extremely valuable course short. To do so will probably result in future difficulties not only in law school, but also in the later practice of law.

II. The Learning Process in General

The learning process, as relates to the study of law, is a matter of comprehension that a rule can be extracted from a decided case, evaluated, generalized consistent with accuracy and finally applied to various specific fact situations in order to test the limits of generalization. This process can be complicated. Perhaps the best way to understand it is to examine its essential elements, which are (1) impression, (2) association, (3) expression and (4) repetition. The net result of the four elements is comprehension. Each of the elements is necessary to the end result, and if one element is excluded from the study program, the student will not learn rapidly enough to keep pace with his or her class.

Impression will normally come from the casebook, but not necessarily limited thereto. Regardless of where the initial impression originates, it must be there to initiate the learning process. The next step is to associate the concept or point with other related material and to contrast it with opposing ideas. Casebooks are traditionally arranged to stimulate association. The naked concept expounded in one case will often take on a new meaning when related to prior and subsequent cases, footnotes and other related material. Association is an aid to memory and essential to comprehension. An idea related to many others will more likely be recalled than one standing alone. Moreover, in studying law you are not merely memorizing history, i.e., what the courts have done; but rather trying to build a working foundation that will allow you to use and apply that information to predict the solution of similar fact situations arising in the future. At this point, the student should be able to express himself with respect to the legal point involved in the studied case. Unless the student can do so, he or she has not comprehended the material. Before completing your law school training, you will hear over and over, "I knew the course, as well as anyone, but I just couldn't express myself on the examination." How well did this student really "know" the course material? In all probability, it is concepts that you envision that are vague or which you have not thoroughly understood that cause you have difficulty in communicating to others, both on an examination paper and during recitation in the classroom. Although storekeepers A and B might have identical inventory items, if one is the better sales person, he or she will reap the greatest rewards. Exactly the same principle applies in law school competition. And if you do not believe anything else, believe that it is competitive. Therefore, practice constantly to improve your ability to express yourself; and remember that although comprehension is the net result of all four elements mentioned above, it is at the same time a requisite to effective expression. The final element of the learning process is repetition. There are but few tasks in life that can be learned the first time that they are encountered. The chances are that you sank, rather than swam, on your first trip to the swimming hole. The ability to comprehend legal material is no different; there must be repeated impressions, associations and expressions to do one's best. Otherwise, our mind will not contain clear and understandable concepts, ideas and answers, but rather a jungle of vague and unusable material.

III. A Suggested Program of Study

A. Reading Cases

Before you can properly read a case, you must understand what it is and know what to look for. Cases are published reports of human controversies and tragedies that have been resolved by our legal processes. They include the court's decision and its reasons for the decision. Normally, the first thing you will find in a case is a statement of the nature of the controversy, how it happens to be before this particular court for decision, and what action was taken in the court below. A statement of the facts surrounding the controversy typically follows. In a well-written decision, the next step in the development of a reported case would be a statement of the issues; i.e., precisely what it is that the court has been called upon to decide. Often these will be expressly delineated, but sometimes they are left to inference from the balance of the opinion. The contentions of both parties usually follow the statement of the issues and are often intertwined with various expressions of the court's reasoning in accepting or rejecting the various arguments advanced by the parties. Finally, the court's general conclusion is stated, followed by a brief statement of the decision, e.g., "Judgment Affirmed," "Reversed and Rendered," "Reversed and Remanded."

Read the case in its entirety before underlining or making any marginal notations. Do so carefully and thoroughly, concentrating on what you read. Premature attempts to reduce your thoughts to writing will likely result in a waste of time. Ask yourself what prompted the editor of the casebook to insert the case in the text at this point. By doing this, you should be able to distinguish between the principal and, if any, irrelevant points. Then reread the case, underlining the most important portions and/or making marginal notations. Remember that the *rule of law* can be used and applied only if one understands the *reasons* necessitating the rule. Make a mental brief of the case without reference to the casebook before reducing it to writing.

B. Briefing Cases

The brief of a case with which a law student is concerned means a brief summary of the case in the *student's own words*. Do not merely quote various portions of the opinion for in all probability, this will mean little by the time you reach the classroom and even less when you begin to review the course at exam time. A good brief means that the student has read and comprehended the significant points therein. It is important not only for class recitations, but also as a permanent *condensed* record for the future.

The form of the brief can be varied in many ways without sacrificing effectiveness; however, a logical beginning student's brief would include:

Action: State here the nature of the controversy as explained above.

Facts: Enumerate the essential facts necessary to the decision.

Issue(s): State the relevant question(s) to be decided by this court.

Holding: State the decision on the point(s) in controversy.

Reasons: State the reasoning that prompted this result.

Rule: State a concise generalization of the principle relevant to your study.

For example, below is a brief of the case which typically initiates the student to the assault and battery section of his casebook on torts:

I DE S. and Wife v. *W DE S.*
At the Assizes, 1348 or 1839

Action: Damages for an assault.

Facts: W came to I's tavern for some wine. Finding the tavern was closed, he struck on its door

	with a hatchet. I's wife put her head out of nearby window; and W struck at, but did not touch, her with his hatchet.
Issue:	(Implied) Is a trespass to the person actionable when the defendant's act does not result in a battery?
Holding:	For the plaintiff, damages awarded.
Reasons:	There can be *harm* even in the absence of a touch.
Rule:	A touch is not a necessary element of an actionable assault.

After the first year, many students discontinue the preparation of formal briefs. They rely mainly on underlining and marginal notations. Whether you should do so will be better known to you at the end of the first year, or possibly sooner, than to anyone else. But if you do decide to discontinue this practice, it might be wise to supplement your underlining with a few concise statements just above the style of each case in order to jog your memory for class recitations and review. For example, in connection with the foregoing case, this might range from "W struck at, but did not touch, the tavern keeper's wife with a hatchet. Held: Damages awarded to the plaintiff; a touch is not a necessary element of an actionable assault;" to "Swinging hatchet at tavern keeper's wife case—touch not essential to actionable assault."

The amount of such information, of course, would depend upon the individual. Consequently, you can find just about as many variations as there are students in the class. Above all, remember that the inability to make an effective brief, regardless of its form, is a result of the student's inability to extract important issues from complicated problems. Naturally, this is a shortcoming that desires considerable attention. To help resolve it, refer back to the material in the prior section concerning the learning process in general.

C. Taking Notes

The taking of good classroom notes cannot be overemphasized. Regardless of how a particular professor conducts the classroom discussion, the reason for taking good notes remains unchanged, i.e., to supplement your individual study. As in briefing cases, various mechanical methods of note taking are available, and you should choose a method by trial and error proves to be the most helpful. A common method will be noted; however, that employs the spiral notebook previously discussed. Most of such notebooks have pages divided by a vertical line that leaves a broad left hand margin. The cases are then briefed on one side, leaving the other side for class notes. This method has the advantage of collecting your briefs and notes in one place. It also tends to reduce the amount of preliminary matter (e.g., case facts, etc.) that the student is tempted to enter in his class notes. Thus, a time-consuming and unduly repetitious practice is avoided.

Other suggestions, based upon the experiences of many, can also be made. Do not, for instance, attempt to write down everything that is said in class, either by the professor or other students. This is impractical, if not impossible. To attempt to do so will result not only in the frequent loss of the thread of discussion, but also in the cluttering of your notes with a lot of trash. Mentally, brief the material as the discussion progresses; then write a condensation in your own words. It can help to skip a line for each separate concept of law and indent, whenever possible, to indicate a transition from one thought to another. Above all, do not lose sight of your objective in taking class notes, *i.e.*, to supplement your individual study with the *important* things said in the classroom.

D. Review

Review is equally as important as preparation. Many feel that it is even more important. But without attempting to resolve their comparative value, it suffices to say that both are essential to your study program. Either can become, however, a "Frankenstein" if not properly controlled. That is, you must be careful not to pass the point of diminishing returns. To aid you in this respect, it will perhaps be best to divide the discussion into various types of review.

Postclass review. As soon as possible after the classroom discussion, the student should review the assigned cases in light of the classroom discussion. The objective of this review is to test your comprehension of the materials covered and to clarify any vagueness discovered in your notes. Any questions remaining unanswered after an examination of your briefs and notes should be noted, and an attempt to ascertain the answers should be made by referring to recommended outside reading materials. If the confusion still exists, the questions should be organized for presentation at the beginning of the next class session, if the professor allows such a procedure.

Preclass review. If possible, a brief review immediately before class of the previous day's notes and the briefs of the currently assigned cases is most helpful. This procedure will make the classroom discussion more meaningful and will probably reduce the amount of information that need be added to your notes. It also provides more repetition which is essential to the learning process.

Postsection review. This review is actually the first major step toward outlining. In you daily study, you tend to think in terms of individual problems. These must be mastered, of course, but you also need to see the course in its broader view. It is at this point where the student really commences to associate concept with concept. General rules are formulated, and the necessary exceptions noted. If you allow the material covered to remain in unclassified form, it will be extremely difficult to use and apply to solve new problems.

E. Outlines

While the actual techniques of outlining are beyond the scope of this paper, it should be noted that this process is largely a matter of expressing the results of your postsection review. It concerns the organization of the course, not merely the condensation of your class notes. Moreover, it is more than mere restatements of the various rules of law encountered. It should include concise statements of the reasons or policies prompting such rules, along with such other comments as are necessary to illustrate the relationship between the various concepts and rules. Try indenting the various divisions and subdivisions as a mechanical aid in highlighting the relationship between larger and subordinate concepts. The best starting point in this respect is the table of contents of your casebook.

Outlining provides repetition, the association of ideas, and is, of course, an expression of your comprehension of the law. The outline, if perfected, should answer every possible examination question. Thus, the reason why "canned" outlines are undesirable should be obvious. No one's outline can take the place of your own. Actually, it would be better to make one even if you threw it away the next day. The experience of extracting principle ideas from complicated subject matter is the important thing. Indeed, the ability to outline is an art. It will only be acquired after much practice; but until this skill is acquired, the student has not really mastered the learning process.

IV. Examinations

If you have mastered the review technique, you have already solved the problem of examination preparation. Your briefs, notes and outlines are by far the best source of materials for examination study. In addition, however, many recommend concluding your review by answering old exam questions. If time permits, this is certainly a valuable method of testing your comprehension of the course materials. But do not sacrifice familiarity with your outline for this procedure.

Law school examinations are of essentially three types: (1) objective, (2) essay and (3) short answer. Most examinations are a combination of at least two of these types. The objective exam is in many respects similar to those you have taken in your undergraduate days; i.e., they test primarily your memory. They are also employed to provide adequate coverage of the course materials and because they are, of course, easy to grade. While most professors deplore their use, they are nevertheless frequently necessitated by the size of our typical law class. The essay exam, on the other hand, is generally recognized as the best testing device. It best approximates the actual conditions of a law office wherein the client lays out his problem, stated in terms of a group of facts, before the lawyer and requests a solution. The essay exam not only tests your memory, but also determines how well you can use and apply the material to the law. The short answer type of examination typically presents a problem and your answer must be confined to a few lines on the exam paper. Thus, it combines some of the advantages of both of the first two types of exam. The remaining suggestions are primarily designed to aid in the writing of an essay exam, it being the most difficult for the average student to master.

First, scan briefly the examination question, noting primarily the problem requirement. Reread the problem and underline the relevant issues. Then organize your answer by means of a brief outline on a separate piece of paper. Good organization is essential to a good answer; and as a rule of thumb, you should spend at least as much time planning your answer as you do in reducing it to writing. Premature writing will usually result in a rambling waste of effort. In writing your answer, a logical approach is to first state the issues involved. Then develop the authorities, pro and con, from the applicable materials that you have studied. Be sure that these are accurate statements of the rules and their underlying reasons. Apply these authorities to the particular facts at hand, arguing logically step by step. Finally, give your conclusion if one is required. The most frequent errors in exam writing are (1) omitting discussion of more than one possible solution; (2) writing in great detail on the general law involved, but failing to apply it to the particular fact situation; (3) discussing the facts in some detail, but never applying the law; and (4) writing such bulky papers that the grader is unable to extract the gist of what has been written. Camouflage is an excellent military aid, but it will seldom work a miracle for the student who is not emotionally and mentally prepared for the examination.

Although emphasis should be placed on conciseness consistent with accuracy, do not leave out essential steps in your reasoning upon the assumption that the professor will know they were necessary to your conclusion. He does not assume you can solve the problem until you have demonstrated that you can. Your answer must be entirely readable. Remember that you, the student, have the burden of persuading the professor that you understand the problem and have arrived at a reasonably satisfactory solution!

V. Conclusion

It is obvious from all of the foregoing that *time* is the most valuable asset in pursuing the study of law. Thus, your primary problem in succeeding in this endeavor is in managing your time in the best and most efficient manner. Budget it wisely in preparing your own study program. Perhaps you will find that you are unable to accomplish an adequate program with the normal law school load. If so, you must make an early decision to sacrifice grades or reduce the number of hours you carry. Finally, it should be emphasized that a good study program should be flexible. If the particular program you adopt does not prove beneficial, do not hesitate to alter it in the light of your accumulated experiences. As is true in most matters, experience is still the best teacher.

Letter Written By Thomas George Deffebach to His Daughter in the Early 1940's About His Christian Beliefs

Dear Beth:

I am writing to you in order that you may understand more nearly how and what your Mother and I believe. To believe what fundamentally it takes to be a Christian, you only need the following brief creed: "I take Jesus, the Christ, God and Son, to be my savior and I will walk in his way."

In the beginning, God created man. He breathed into Adam the "Breath of Life" and Adam became a living soul. The reason why God created man is not entirely clear to us while still "still in the flesh", because in this life we see through a glass darkly due to our lack of spiritual development. It is evident that He had a great purpose in mind that will be revealed to us in God's good time.

He created Adam and placed him in the Garden; intending, at the proper time, to endow him with the knowledge of good & evil. Adam and Eve tasted before God was ready for them to receive this knowledge and their sin of disobedience brought on its own punishment. I have no doubt that God intended at the proper time to reveal to them the knowledge of good and evil. It was necessary for man, in his spiritual development, to possess this knowledge and for him to meet and overcome temptations in order that he might grow strong spiritually. There is no other way for man to grow strong except by overcoming. This is the great lesson of the Book of Revelation.

To bring about this growth, God gave man the necessary free will, so that he becomes a moral individual. The bird cares for her young in the nest until his wings are strong and it is time for him to learn to fly. Then the mother bird, because she loves the birdling and wants him to develop, pushes him out of the nest and it flies.

The perfection of Adam was only the perfection of innocence—the perfection of a babe. The goal for man as set by God in the Scriptures, is to measure up to the perfection of the man Christ Jesus. Man is an individual and his progress is individual first, and next as a part of church and state.

The religion of ancient Israel was mainly in mass. They had a great leader and they did that which was right in the sight of God. They had a wicked ruler and they did the reverse. If the love of God had dwelt in each individual heart they would have served the Lord, even under unfavorable conditions. This was totalitarianism and the world has seen too much of it even in modern times. Its results were only partial under the good leaders. A few great souls such as Moses, Abraham, Joseph and David towered above the masses, but the masses did not make much spiritual progress. Christ began to build by individuals primarily. He called Peter, James, John and Paul. He said "the Kingdom of God is within you" as well as the kingdom of darkness. He drove out the devils that dwelt in the human heart so that the light of Christ could enter. "The light shown in the darkness and darkness comprehended it not." This light wrought destruction in the way Abraham Lincoln destroyed his enemies. It is said that during the Civil War a lady criticized the great President by saying that he extended aid to many of his enemies when he should have destroyed them. He answered: "Lady, I destroy them by making friends of them." In this way, evil will finally be destroyed out of the universe. "And the devil and hell will be cast into the Lake of Fire."

We are born one by one. We pass through the great change which we call death, one by one. There is a natural body and there is a spiritual one. We do not get the spirited body when we die, but we have it now. When the change we call death comes, we go straight to the Judgment in the spiritual world. This happens one by one and it is happening all the time. The Judgment Day is a continuing day. This great day which is described in the 24th chapter of Matthew is also the second coming of Christ and the resurrection day of the soul.

Christ will never come back to the earth in the flesh. When we see him again, he will be spiritual and we will be spiritual. The soul does not sleep in the grave. "And the body shall return to the dust of the earth and the soul to God who gave it." Christ told the dying thief: "This day thou shalt be with me in paradise." Life is continuous. The soul (the real self) never dies."

Punishment is "age lasting" and its purpose is redemptive. "Whom the Lord loveth he chastened. The purpose of the Lord's punishment, administered in Love, is redemptive for we are his children. When we have been drawn by the "cords of love" into harmony with His will, the punishment will cease. It may be only a short time and it may, in some cases, take ages. While it lasts we are in Hell.

The Kingdom of God will finally prevail upon the earth. Then earth will be a part of Heaven. Death is a glorious transformation. We should look forward to it with joy as a time when we will be free from the limitations of the flesh, free to understand and take part in the great spiritual activities of that other world for which the Lord is preparing us for, here and now.

Beth, we have found great joy and comfort in the above beliefs. I am not saying I expect you to believe this like we do. If you ever accept it all, you will grow into it. I shall say nothing more to you about it unless you wish to ask me any questions concerning any part of it.

Love, Dad

TO RENE WITH LOVE

On Sabbath morn she kept the door
And welcomed people in.
Her laughing voice gave words of cheer,
A loving thought that was sincere.
A place of God was made more dear
As holy day began.

It mattered not how cold the morn
Her faithful stance she took.
The heavy door she opened wide,
A warm handclasp drew souls inside,
The eager ones for Him to guide,
By words from the sacred book.

Me thinks that on the Judgment Day,
When earth no more we roam,
Perchance He'll let his servant dear
Stand by a door again with cheer
To greet His children far and near
Into the Heavenly Home!

—Rose Deffebach